I0114026

Moon method
Diary
2021

© COPYRIGHT ANNA MARIA WHITEHEAD 2021

LUNAR CALENDAR 2021

JANUARY
FEBRUARY
MARCH
APRIL
MAY
JUNE
JULY
AUGUST
SEPTEMBER
OCTOBER
NOVEMBER
DECEMBER

NEW MOON
FIRST QUARTER
FULL MOON
LAST QUARTER

© Tartilastock

'What you think, you become.
What you feel, you attract.
What you imagine, you create.'

— Buddha

2021

January

Sun	Mon	Tue	Wed	Thu	Fri	Sat
					1	2
3	4	5	6	7	8	9
10	11	12	13	14	15	16
17	18	19	20	21	22	23
24	25	26	27	28	29	30
31						

February

Sun	Mon	Tue	Wed	Thu	Fri	Sat
	1	2	3	4	5	6
7	8	9	10	11	12	13
14	15	16	17	18	19	20
21	22	23	24	25	26	27
28						

March

Sun	Mon	Tue	Wed	Thu	Fri	Sat
	1	2	3	4	5	6
7	8	9	10	11	12	13
14	15	16	17	18	19	20
21	22	23	24	25	26	27
28	29	30	31			

April

Sun	Mon	Tue	Wed	Thu	Fri	Sat
				1	2	3
4	5	6	7	8	9	10
11	12	13	14	15	16	17
18	19	20	21	22	23	24
25	26	27	28	29	30	

May

Sun	Mon	Tue	Wed	Thu	Fri	Sat
						1
2	3	4	5	6	7	8
9	10	11	12	13	14	15
16	17	18	19	20	21	22
23	24	25	26	27	28	29
30	31					

June

Sun	Mon	Tue	Wed	Thu	Fri	Sat
		1	2	3	4	5
6	7	8	9	10	11	12
13	14	15	16	17	18	19
20	21	22	23	24	25	26
27	28	29	30			

July

Sun	Mon	Tue	Wed	Thu	Fri	Sat
				1	2	3
4	5	6	7	8	9	10
11	12	13	14	15	16	17
18	19	20	21	22	23	24
25	26	27	28	29	30	31

August

Sun	Mon	Tue	Wed	Thu	Fri	Sat
1	2	3	4	5	6	7
8	9	10	11	12	13	14
15	16	17	18	19	20	21
22	23	24	25	26	27	28
29	30	31				

September

Sun	Mon	Tue	Wed	Thu	Fri	Sat
			1	2	3	4
5	6	7	8	9	10	11
12	13	14	15	16	17	18
19	20	21	22	23	24	25
26	27	28	29	30		

October

Sun	Mon	Tue	Wed	Thu	Fri	Sat
					1	2
3	4	5	6	7	8	9
10	11	12	13	14	15	16
17	18	19	20	21	22	23
24	25	26	27	28	29	30
31						

November

Sun	Mon	Tue	Wed	Thu	Fri	Sat
	1	2	3	4	5	6
7	8	9	10	11	12	13
14	15	16	17	18	19	20
21	22	23	24	25	26	27
28	29	30				

December

Sun	Mon	Tue	Wed	Thu	Fri	Sat
			1	2	3	4
5	6	7	8	9	10	11
12	13	14	15	16	17	18
19	20	21	22	23	24	25
26	27	28	29	30	31	

May the Sun bring you new energy by day.
May the Moon softly restore you by night.
May the rain wash away your worries.
May the breeze blow strength into your being.
May you walk gently through the world and
know its beauty all the days of your life.
- Apache Blessing

Created by Anna Maria Whitehead
Design by Erica Cooper

Phases of the moon

New Moon
New beginnings and intention setting

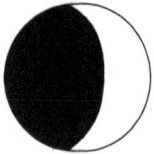

Waxing Moon
Put plans into action

Full Moon
Gratitude for all you have received

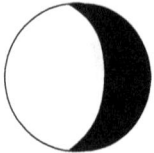

Waning Moon
Release anything that no longer serves you

Working with the moon

Live in sync with nature to manifest your best life.

Do you ever feel overwhelmed with to-do lists? Do you experience days when you have planned to see a friend, only to find when the day comes along you do not feel like socialising?

The secret is being able to forward plan our schedules by having an idea of where our energy levels will be at different times throughout the month. Nature can help you to be your most productive self. Use the varying energy of the moon's cycles to your benefit. The demands of our modern world often make us feel that we need to be on top of our game every day. Being busy is almost treated as a badge of honour, but we are not supposed to be operating at one hundred percent every day of the month. We are cyclical beings. Rest and time spent alone also need to be honoured and included on our schedules with the same importance as any business meeting.

When we rest, we re-charge and become our most productive selves. During the New Moon we set intentions for the month ahead, we are then free to move forward focussing on our goals, with a renewed clarity on what we want and heightened energy to get us there.

The aim of this diary is to help you to organise busy schedules whilst avoiding burnout and feeling overwhelmed. When life flows easily, creativity and happiness will come to you in abundance.

Wishing you a very happy, productive year full of joy.

A **New Moon** is a monthly rebirth, a time for new beginnings, ideas and creativity. An opportunity to set your intentions. This is a perfect time to spend alone journaling your thoughts and practicing self care which will mean different things to all of you. Perhaps a morning meditation or an evening bubble bath is all it takes, but whatever it is, make sure to take some time for yourself. In the silence you will receive the intuitive guidance you need. Take some time to set your intentions for the month ahead.

Crystal recommendation: *Clear Quartz*, a cleansing crystal perfect for clearing the mind and aiding in meditation.

The **Waxing Moon** asks you to act upon the ideas you received during the new moon. This is a perfect time for socialising and communication, so scheduling in meetings would be good during a waxing moon, but be careful not to burnout, eat well during this moon and avoid anything not so good for you.

Citrine, a wonderful crystal for manifesting abundance.

A **Full Moon** is when you check in with the intentions you set under the new moon. Consider what finishing touches you need to look at to get you to your goals. Work with your intuition and gut feelings. Energies are very high under this powerful moon phase, so you will have energy for meeting with friends, but you may prefer to use this energy to be at home burning your favourite incense whilst meditating and tuning into your highest self. Full moons are a great time to cleanse the body and mind.

Moonstone, helps to connect to your inner goddess and true meaning.

The **Waning Moon** calls you to release that which does not serve you. Pay attention to anything that has stood in the way of your goals and dreams. This is a perfect time to organise, throw things away, consider if you have any toxic elements in your life, do you need to get rid of any particular bad habits? Now would be the time to start looking at that. Let go of unwanted energy and release .

Rhodonite, a healer related to the heart chakra which helps with forgiveness and releases self-destructive tendencies to help with healing at a soul level.

How amazing is the moon!? She provides us with the chance to start afresh every month and use her energy to guide us.

A little side note about working with and charting menstrual cycles along side the moon cycles:

Start on day 1 of your menstrual cycle and write a note on each day about anything you feel you would like to chart, particularly your emotions and energy levels.

It is good practice to chart our cycles, and this includes those of us who don't have a menstrual cycle. It can still be very beneficial to chart our states of being on a daily basis allowing us to notice any patterns over the period of a few months. This is a useful tool in getting to know subtleties about yourself. You can then use this information to work in harmony with your inner ebs and flows. For example if you see that you are always exhausted on day 5, but full of life on day 12 then you can use this information to your advantage.

Honouring the seasons

Paying close attention to the seasons and creating rituals around them helps us in turn to honour ourselves. We are nature. We are cyclic beings. When we move with the natural rhythms of our Earth, we learn to live in a flow state, in the present. As each season moves into the next on the wheel of the year, we can celebrate these changes outside and inside of ourselves. Equinoxes and solstices allow us to feel at one with the seasons and remind us to check in with ourselves, so rather than mindlessly racing through the year wondering how another one flew by so quickly, working with the seasons can add focus and clarity to those 365 days.

Spring equinox 20th March

A time when light and dark come into balance and nature blooms with life. Use this time to think about what seeds you want to sow in your own life. How do you want to use this new vital energy to manifest abundance? Spring shows us how to be patient whilst we wait for the little buds to blossom. Emulate nature in this way and be easy on yourself if you are waiting for your manifestations to come to fruition. Try and spend at least ten minutes every day with your bare feet touching the Earth. Take as much time in nature as you can, pausing to pay attention to spring as she emerges from the dark winter. Close your eyes and take in the sounds of nature all around you. Spend time journaling on your goals for the remainder of the year. Are there steps you can now take as you leave winter behind you to get ready to step into the light of spring.

Ritual ideas: Cleanse your space with frankincense or incense of your choice, do a grounding meditation such as a root chakra meditation by imagining that your feet root firmly into the Earth, you could sit with your back against a tree for twenty minutes connecting with the Earths energy, followed by a cleansing bath with epsom salts and rose petals.

Summer solstice 21st June

In the northern hemisphere the Earth's axis is tilted at its closest point from the sun. This is the longest day, and shortest night. Nature is in full bloom all around us and inspires us to put our creative ideas in practice and bring projects to life. Use the heightened energy of the solstice to create and be inspired.

Ritual Ideas: Get outside, run barefoot with flowers in your hair, hold all night bonfires with friends. Celebrate nature and each other. Eat fresh food from the Earth and give thanks for all that she provides us. Write lists of everything you are grateful for. What is showing up in abundance for you? Stop and pause to give thanks for it. Get up at sunrise to honour the sun. Perhaps enjoy a yoga session on a beach at sunrise. Get creative with your celebrations and make them your own.

Autumn equinox 22nd September
The first day of autumn is a time for releasing. Get clear on what no longer serves you, and just like the trees who shed their leaves, allow yourself to let go. The days will begin to get shorter and nature invites you to retreat inwards to rejuvenate. There is a different level of energy that we are now heading into, and one of the best ways to honour that time is to reflect on the year so far, and ask what you need to shed to move forward.

Ritual ideas: Write a list of anything you don't want to take with you as we move into this next part of the year. You could have a bonfire and burn the list. Take a long walk and notice the changes in nature all around you and take home some moss and wood to make an alter for the Earth goddess Gaia. As the nights get shorter and the air gets colder embrace the change in energy and the subtle whispers calling you inwards.

Winter solstice 21st December
Celebrate the cyclical nature of our world on the longest night before the sun is renewed once more. The winter solstice welcomes a slower pace, honour that. The darkness of winter can be difficult, try and notice the beauty of the sparse trees and frosty mornings. Treat yourself to comforting foods and special time with loved ones playing board games and embrace the slower, quieter, darker days.

Ritual ideas: Spend some time in silence reflecting on the year so far and your dreams for the year ahead. Head to a beauty spot that you have a connection with and reflect on any changes to this area during winter. Wrap up warm and enjoy a fire, the flames can be very meditative and healing. Shamans say that fire allows for rapid transformation. Make the most of the darkness and any revelations it has helped to bring to light.

Goals for 2021

Use this space to write your goals for the year ahead,
and any steps you can take that will get you to where you
want to be.

Vision board

Use this space to paint, doodle or cut pictures out
of magazines. Whatever works for you. The goal is to create
a powerful visualization tool to aid in manifesting your
dreams. You can look at this every day to bring your
2021 goals to life.

January 2021

Notes	Monday	Tuesday	Wednesday
			30
	4	5	6 ◗
	11	12	13 ●
	18	19	20 ◖
	25	26	27

Thursday	Friday	Saturday	Sunday
31	1	2	3
7	8	9	10
14	15	16	17
21	22	23	24
28 ◯	29	30	31

January
Wolf moon

January goals

Use this space to write your goals for the month ahead, and any steps you can take that will get you to where you want to be.

Friday | 1 January 2021

6:00	**Today's quick wins**
7:00	
8:00	
9:00	
10:00	
11:00	**Health and nutrition**
12:00	
13:00	
14:00	**Today, I am grateful for...**
15:00	
16:00	
17:00	**Today's self care**
18:00	
19:00	
20:00	**Chart your cycle**
21:00	
22:00	
23:00	**Positive affirmation**
Notes	

Saturday | 2 January 2021

6:00	**Today's quick wins**
7:00	
8:00	
9:00	
10:00	
11:00	**Health and nutrition**
12:00	
13:00	
14:00	**Today, I am grateful for...**
15:00	
16:00	
17:00	**Today's self care**
18:00	
19:00	
20:00	**Chart your cycle**
21:00	
22:00	
23:00	**Positive affirmation**
Notes	

Sunday | 3 January 2021

6:00	**Today's quick wins**
7:00	
8:00	
9:00	
10:00	
11:00	**Health and nutrition**
12:00	
13:00	
14:00	**Today, I am grateful for...**
15:00	
16:00	
17:00	**Today's self care**
18:00	
19:00	
20:00	**Chart your cycle**
21:00	
22:00	
23:00	**Positive affirmation**
Notes	

Wednesday | 6 January 2021

6:00	
7:00	
8:00	
9:00	
10:00	
11:00	
12:00	
13:00	
14:00	
15:00	
16:00	
17:00	
18:00	
19:00	
20:00	
21:00	
22:00	
23:00	

Notes

Today's quick wins

Health and nutrition

Today, I am grateful for...

Today's self care

Chart your cycle

Positive affirmation

Thursday | 7 January 2021

6:00	**Today's quick wins**
7:00	
8:00	
9:00	
10:00	
11:00	**Health and nutrition**
12:00	
13:00	
14:00	**Today, I am grateful for...**
15:00	
16:00	
17:00	**Today's self care**
18:00	
19:00	
20:00	**Chart your cycle**
21:00	
22:00	
23:00	**Positive affirmation**
Notes	

Friday | 8 January 2021

6:00	**Today's quick wins**
7:00	
8:00	
9:00	
10:00	
11:00	**Health and nutrition**
12:00	
13:00	
14:00	**Today, I am grateful for...**
15:00	
16:00	
17:00	**Today's self care**
18:00	
19:00	
20:00	**Chart your cycle**
21:00	
22:00	
23:00	**Positive affirmation**
Notes	

Saturday | 9 January 2021

6:00	**Today's quick wins**
7:00	
8:00	
9:00	
10:00	
11:00	**Health and nutrition**
12:00	
13:00	
14:00	**Today, I am grateful for...**
15:00	
16:00	
17:00	**Today's self care**
18:00	
19:00	
20:00	**Chart your cycle**
21:00	
22:00	
23:00	**Positive affirmation**
Notes	

Sunday | 10 January 2021

6:00	**Today's quick wins**
7:00	
8:00	
9:00	
10:00	
11:00	**Health and nutrition**
12:00	
13:00	
14:00	**Today, I am grateful for...**
15:00	
16:00	
17:00	**Today's self care**
18:00	
19:00	
20:00	**Chart your cycle**
21:00	
22:00	
23:00	**Positive affirmation**
Notes	

Monday | 11 January 2021

6:00	
7:00	
8:00	
9:00	
10:00	
11:00	
12:00	
13:00	
14:00	
15:00	
16:00	
17:00	
18:00	
19:00	
20:00	
21:00	
22:00	
23:00	

Today's quick wins

Health and nutrition

Today, I am grateful for...

Today's self care

Chart your cycle

Positive affirmation

Notes

Tuesday | 12 January 2021

6:00	**Today's quick wins**
7:00	
8:00	
9:00	
10:00	
11:00	**Health and nutrition**
12:00	
13:00	
14:00	**Today, I am grateful for...**
15:00	
16:00	
17:00	**Today's self care**
18:00	
19:00	
20:00	**Chart your cycle**
21:00	
22:00	
23:00	**Positive affirmation**
Notes	

Wednesday | 13 January 2021

6:00	
7:00	
8:00	
9:00	
10:00	
11:00	
12:00	
13:00	
14:00	
15:00	
16:00	
17:00	
18:00	
19:00	
20:00	
21:00	
22:00	
23:00	

Today's quick wins

Health and nutrition

Today, I am grateful for...

Today's self care

Chart your cycle

Positive affirmation

Notes

Thursday | 14 January 2021

6:00	**Today's quick wins**
7:00	
8:00	
9:00	
10:00	
11:00	**Health and nutrition**
12:00	
13:00	
14:00	**Today, I am grateful for...**
15:00	
16:00	
17:00	**Today's self care**
18:00	
19:00	
20:00	**Chart your cycle**
21:00	
22:00	
23:00	**Positive affirmation**
Notes	

Friday | 15 January 2021

6:00	**Today's quick wins**
7:00	
8:00	
9:00	
10:00	
11:00	**Health and nutrition**
12:00	
13:00	
14:00	**Today, I am grateful for...**
15:00	
16:00	
17:00	**Today's self care**
18:00	
19:00	
20:00	**Chart your cycle**
21:00	
22:00	
23:00	**Positive affirmation**
Notes	

Saturday | 16 January 2021

6:00	**Today's quick wins**
7:00	
8:00	
9:00	
10:00	
11:00	**Health and nutrition**
12:00	
13:00	
14:00	**Today, I am grateful for...**
15:00	
16:00	
17:00	**Today's self care**
18:00	
19:00	
20:00	**Chart your cycle**
21:00	
22:00	
23:00	**Positive affirmation**
Notes	

Sunday | 17 January 2021

6:00	
7:00	
8:00	
9:00	
10:00	
11:00	
12:00	
13:00	
14:00	
15:00	
16:00	
17:00	
18:00	
19:00	
20:00	
21:00	
22:00	
23:00	

Today's quick wins

Health and nutrition

Today, I am grateful for...

Today's self care

Chart your cycle

Positive affirmation

Notes

Monday | 18 January 2021

6:00	
7:00	
8:00	
9:00	
10:00	
11:00	
12:00	
13:00	
14:00	
15:00	
16:00	
17:00	
18:00	
19:00	
20:00	
21:00	
22:00	
23:00	

Today's quick wins

Health and nutrition

Today, I am grateful for...

Today's self care

Chart your cycle

Positive affirmation

Notes

Tuesday | 19 January 2021

6:00	**Today's quick wins**
7:00	
8:00	
9:00	
10:00	
11:00	**Health and nutrition**
12:00	
13:00	
14:00	**Today, I am grateful for...**
15:00	
16:00	
17:00	**Today's self care**
18:00	
19:00	
20:00	**Chart your cycle**
21:00	
22:00	
23:00	**Positive affirmation**
Notes	

Wednesday | 20 January 2021

6:00	**Today's quick wins**
7:00	
8:00	
9:00	
10:00	
11:00	**Health and nutrition**
12:00	
13:00	
14:00	**Today, I am grateful for...**
15:00	
16:00	
17:00	**Today's self care**
18:00	
19:00	
20:00	**Chart your cycle**
21:00	
22:00	
23:00	**Positive affirmation**
Notes	

Thursday | 21 January 2021

6:00	**Today's quick wins**
7:00	
8:00	
9:00	
10:00	
11:00	**Health and nutrition**
12:00	
13:00	
14:00	**Today, I am grateful for...**
15:00	
16:00	
17:00	**Today's self care**
18:00	
19:00	
20:00	**Chart your cycle**
21:00	
22:00	
23:00	**Positive affirmation**
Notes	

Friday | 22 January 2021

6:00	**Today's quick wins**
7:00	
8:00	
9:00	
10:00	
11:00	**Health and nutrition**
12:00	
13:00	
14:00	**Today, I am grateful for...**
15:00	
16:00	
17:00	**Today's self care**
18:00	
19:00	
20:00	**Chart your cycle**
21:00	
22:00	
23:00	**Positive affirmation**
Notes	

6:00	**Today's quick wins**
7:00	
8:00	
9:00	
10:00	
11:00	**Health and nutrition**
12:00	
13:00	
14:00	**Today, I am grateful for...**
15:00	
16:00	
17:00	**Today's self care**
18:00	
19:00	
20:00	**Chart your cycle**
21:00	
22:00	
23:00	**Positive affirmation**
Notes	

Sunday | 24 January 2021

6:00	**Today's quick wins**
7:00	
8:00	
9:00	
10:00	
11:00	**Health and nutrition**
12:00	
13:00	
14:00	**Today, I am grateful for...**
15:00	
16:00	
17:00	**Today's self care**
18:00	
19:00	
20:00	**Chart your cycle**
21:00	
22:00	
23:00	**Positive affirmation**
Notes	

Monday | 25 January 2021

6:00	**Today's quick wins**
7:00	
8:00	
9:00	
10:00	
11:00	**Health and nutrition**
12:00	
13:00	
14:00	**Today, I am grateful for...**
15:00	
16:00	
17:00	**Today's self care**
18:00	
19:00	
20:00	**Chart your cycle**
21:00	
22:00	
23:00	**Positive affirmation**
Notes	

Tuesday | 26 January 2021

6:00	**Today's quick wins**
7:00	
8:00	
9:00	
10:00	
11:00	**Health and nutrition**
12:00	
13:00	
14:00	**Today, I am grateful for...**
15:00	
16:00	
17:00	**Today's self care**
18:00	
19:00	
20:00	**Chart your cycle**
21:00	
22:00	
23:00	**Positive affirmation**
Notes	

Wednesday | 27 January 2021

6:00	
7:00	
8:00	
9:00	
10:00	
11:00	
12:00	
13:00	
14:00	
15:00	
16:00	
17:00	
18:00	
19:00	
20:00	
21:00	
22:00	
23:00	

Notes

Today's quick wins

Health and nutrition

Today, I am grateful for...

Today's self care

Chart your cycle

Positive affirmation

Thursday | 28 January 2021

6:00	
7:00	
8:00	
9:00	
10:00	
11:00	
12:00	
13:00	
14:00	
15:00	
16:00	
17:00	
18:00	
19:00	
20:00	
21:00	
22:00	
23:00	

Today's quick wins

Health and nutrition

Today, I am grateful for...

Today's self care

Chart your cycle

Positive affirmation

Notes

Friday | 29 January 2021

6:00	
7:00	
8:00	
9:00	
10:00	
11:00	
12:00	
13:00	
14:00	
15:00	
16:00	
17:00	
18:00	
19:00	
20:00	
21:00	
22:00	
23:00	
Notes	

Today's quick wins

Health and nutrition

Today, I am grateful for...

Today's self care

Chart your cycle

Positive affirmation

Saturday | 30 January 2021

6:00	**Today's quick wins**
7:00	
8:00	
9:00	
10:00	
11:00	**Health and nutrition**
12:00	
13:00	
14:00	**Today, I am grateful for...**
15:00	
16:00	
17:00	**Today's self care**
18:00	
19:00	
20:00	**Chart your cycle**
21:00	
22:00	
23:00	**Positive affirmation**
Notes	

Sunday | 31 January 2021

6:00	**Today's quick wins**
7:00	
8:00	
9:00	
10:00	
11:00	**Health and nutrition**
12:00	
13:00	
14:00	**Today, I am grateful for...**
15:00	
16:00	
17:00	**Today's self care**
18:00	
19:00	
20:00	**Chart your cycle**
21:00	
22:00	
23:00	**Positive affirmation**
Notes	

January achievements

Be proud of yourself and all that you have achieved this month. Write down your wins, big and small. If you have not achieved everything that you set out to do, that's okay! We learn and grow through our mistakes and experiences. You can use this space to make notes about anything that you have learned.

February 2021

Notes	Monday	Tuesday	Wednesday
	1	2	3
	8	9	10
	15	16	17
	22	23	24

Thursday	Friday	Saturday	Sunday
4 ☽	5	6	7
11 ●	12	13	14
18	19 ☾	20	21
25	26	27 ○	28
4	5	6	7v

February

Snow moon

February goals

Use this space to write your goals for the month ahead, and any steps you can take that will get you to where you want to be.

'Let yourself be drawn by the strange pull of what you love. It will not lead you astray.'

– Rumi

Use this space to make some notes about your passions, and ask yourself, are you doing what you love? If not, what steps can you take to move closer to your dreams?

Monday | 1 February 2021

6:00	**Today's quick wins**
7:00	
8:00	
9:00	
10:00	
11:00	**Health and nutrition**
12:00	
13:00	
14:00	**Today, I am grateful for...**
15:00	
16:00	
17:00	**Today's self care**
18:00	
19:00	
20:00	**Chart your cycle**
21:00	
22:00	
23:00	**Positive affirmation**
Notes	

Tuesday | 2 February 2021

6:00	**Today's quick wins**
7:00	
8:00	
9:00	
10:00	
11:00	**Health and nutrition**
12:00	
13:00	
14:00	**Today, I am grateful for...**
15:00	
16:00	
17:00	**Today's self care**
18:00	
19:00	
20:00	**Chart your cycle**
21:00	
22:00	
23:00	**Positive affirmation**
Notes	

Wednesday | 3 February 2021

6:00	**Today's quick wins**
7:00	
8:00	
9:00	
10:00	
11:00	**Health and nutrition**
12:00	
13:00	
14:00	**Today, I am grateful for...**
15:00	
16:00	
17:00	**Today's self care**
18:00	
19:00	
20:00	**Chart your cycle**
21:00	
22:00	
23:00	**Positive affirmation**
Notes	

Thursday | 4 February 2021

6:00	**Today's quick wins**
7:00	
8:00	
9:00	
10:00	
11:00	**Health and nutrition**
12:00	
13:00	
14:00	**Today, I am grateful for...**
15:00	
16:00	
17:00	**Today's self care**
18:00	
19:00	
20:00	**Chart your cycle**
21:00	
22:00	
23:00	**Positive affirmation**
Notes	

Friday | 5 February 2021

6:00	**Today's quick wins**
7:00	
8:00	
9:00	
10:00	
11:00	**Health and nutrition**
12:00	
13:00	
14:00	**Today, I am grateful for...**
15:00	
16:00	
17:00	**Today's self care**
18:00	
19:00	
20:00	**Chart your cycle**
21:00	
22:00	
23:00	**Positive affirmation**
Notes	

Saturday | 6 February 2021

6:00	
7:00	
8:00	
9:00	
10:00	
11:00	
12:00	
13:00	
14:00	
15:00	
16:00	
17:00	
18:00	
19:00	
20:00	
21:00	
22:00	
23:00	

Today's quick wins

Health and nutrition

Today, I am grateful for...

Today's self care

Chart your cycle

Positive affirmation

Notes

Sunday | 7 February 2021

6:00	**Today's quick wins**
7:00	
8:00	
9:00	
10:00	
11:00	**Health and nutrition**
12:00	
13:00	
14:00	**Today, I am grateful for...**
15:00	
16:00	
17:00	**Today's self care**
18:00	
19:00	
20:00	**Chart your cycle**
21:00	
22:00	
23:00	**Positive affirmation**
Notes	

Monday | 8 February 2021

6:00	
7:00	
8:00	
9:00	
10:00	
11:00	
12:00	
13:00	
14:00	
15:00	
16:00	
17:00	
18:00	
19:00	
20:00	
21:00	
22:00	
23:00	

Notes

Today's quick wins

Health and nutrition

Today, I am grateful for...

Today's self care

Chart your cycle

Positive affirmation

Tuesday | 9 February 2021

6:00	**Today's quick wins**
7:00	
8:00	
9:00	
10:00	
11:00	**Health and nutrition**
12:00	
13:00	
14:00	**Today, I am grateful for...**
15:00	
16:00	
17:00	**Today's self care**
18:00	
19:00	
20:00	**Chart your cycle**
21:00	
22:00	
23:00	**Positive affirmation**
Notes	

Wednesday | 10 February 2021

6:00	**Today's quick wins**
7:00	
8:00	
9:00	
10:00	
11:00	**Health and nutrition**
12:00	
13:00	
14:00	**Today, I am grateful for...**
15:00	
16:00	
17:00	**Today's self care**
18:00	
19:00	
20:00	**Chart your cycle**
21:00	
22:00	
23:00	**Positive affirmation**
Notes	

Thursday | 11 February 2021

6:00	
7:00	
8:00	
9:00	
10:00	
11:00	
12:00	
13:00	
14:00	
15:00	
16:00	
17:00	
18:00	
19:00	
20:00	
21:00	
22:00	
23:00	

Today's quick wins

Health and nutrition

Today, I am grateful for...

Today's self care

Chart your cycle

Positive affirmation

Notes

Friday | 12 February 2021

6:00	
7:00	
8:00	
9:00	
10:00	
11:00	
12:00	
13:00	
14:00	
15:00	
16:00	
17:00	
18:00	
19:00	
20:00	
21:00	
22:00	
23:00	

Today's quick wins

Health and nutrition

Today, I am grateful for...

Today's self care

Chart your cycle

Positive affirmation

Notes

Saturday | 13 February 2021

6:00	**Today's quick wins**
7:00	
8:00	
9:00	
10:00	
11:00	**Health and nutrition**
12:00	
13:00	
14:00	**Today, I am grateful for...**
15:00	
16:00	
17:00	**Today's self care**
18:00	
19:00	
20:00	**Chart your cycle**
21:00	
22:00	
23:00	**Positive affirmation**
Notes	

Sunday | 14 February 2021

6:00	
7:00	
8:00	
9:00	
10:00	
11:00	
12:00	
13:00	
14:00	
15:00	
16:00	
17:00	
18:00	
19:00	
20:00	
21:00	
22:00	
23:00	

Today's quick wins

Health and nutrition

Today, I am grateful for...

Today's self care

Chart your cycle

Positive affirmation

Notes

Monday | 15 January 2021

6:00	
7:00	
8:00	
9:00	
10:00	
11:00	
12:00	
13:00	
14:00	
15:00	
16:00	
17:00	
18:00	
19:00	
20:00	
21:00	
22:00	
23:00	

Today's quick wins

Health and nutrition

Today, I am grateful for...

Today's self care

Chart your cycle

Positive affirmation

Notes

Tuesday | 16 February 2021

6:00	**Today's quick wins**
7:00	
8:00	
9:00	
10:00	
11:00	**Health and nutrition**
12:00	
13:00	
14:00	**Today, I am grateful for...**
15:00	
16:00	
17:00	**Today's self care**
18:00	
19:00	
20:00	**Chart your cycle**
21:00	
22:00	
23:00	**Positive affirmation**
Notes	

Wednesday | 17 February 2021

6:00	**Today's quick wins**
7:00	
8:00	
9:00	
10:00	
11:00	**Health and nutrition**
12:00	
13:00	
14:00	**Today, I am grateful for...**
15:00	
16:00	
17:00	**Today's self care**
18:00	
19:00	
20:00	**Chart your cycle**
21:00	
22:00	
23:00	**Positive affirmation**
Notes	

Thursday | 18 February 2021

6:00		**Today's quick wins**
7:00		
8:00		
9:00		
10:00		
11:00		**Health and nutrition**
12:00		
13:00		
14:00		**Today, I am grateful for...**
15:00		
16:00		
17:00		**Today's self care**
18:00		
19:00		
20:00		**Chart your cycle**
21:00		
22:00		
23:00		**Positive affirmation**
Notes		

Friday | 19 February 2021

6:00	**Today's quick wins**
7:00	
8:00	
9:00	
10:00	
11:00	**Health and nutrition**
12:00	
13:00	
14:00	**Today, I am grateful for...**
15:00	
16:00	
17:00	**Today's self care**
18:00	
19:00	
20:00	**Chart your cycle**
21:00	
22:00	
23:00	**Positive affirmation**
Notes	

Saturday | 20 February 2021

6:00	**Today's quick wins**	
7:00		
8:00		
9:00		
10:00		
11:00	**Health and nutrition**	
12:00		
13:00		
14:00	**Today, I am grateful for...**	
15:00		
16:00		
17:00	**Today's self care**	
18:00		
19:00		
20:00	**Chart your cycle**	
21:00		
22:00		
23:00	**Positive affirmation**	
Notes		

Sunday | 21 February 2021

6:00	**Today's quick wins**
7:00	
8:00	
9:00	
10:00	
11:00	**Health and nutrition**
12:00	
13:00	
14:00	**Today, I am grateful for...**
15:00	
16:00	
17:00	**Today's self care**
18:00	
19:00	
20:00	**Chart your cycle**
21:00	
22:00	
23:00	**Positive affirmation**
Notes	

Monday | 22 February 2021

6:00	**Today's quick wins**
7:00	
8:00	
9:00	
10:00	
11:00	**Health and nutrition**
12:00	
13:00	
14:00	**Today, I am grateful for...**
15:00	
16:00	
17:00	**Today's self care**
18:00	
19:00	
20:00	**Chart your cycle**
21:00	
22:00	
23:00	**Positive affirmation**
Notes	

Tuesday | 23 February 2021

6:00	**Today's quick wins**
7:00	
8:00	
9:00	
10:00	
11:00	**Health and nutrition**
12:00	
13:00	
14:00	**Today, I am grateful for...**
15:00	
16:00	
17:00	**Today's self care**
18:00	
19:00	
20:00	**Chart your cycle**
21:00	
22:00	
23:00	**Positive affirmation**
Notes	

Wednesday | 24 February 2021

6:00	
7:00	
8:00	
9:00	
10:00	
11:00	
12:00	
13:00	
14:00	
15:00	
16:00	
17:00	
18:00	
19:00	
20:00	
21:00	
22:00	
23:00	
Notes	

Today's quick wins

Health and nutrition

Today, I am grateful for...

Today's self care

Chart your cycle

Positive affirmation

Thursday | 25 February 2021

6:00	**Today's quick wins**
7:00	
8:00	
9:00	
10:00	
11:00	**Health and nutrition**
12:00	
13:00	
14:00	**Today, I am grateful for...**
15:00	
16:00	
17:00	**Today's self care**
18:00	
19:00	
20:00	**Chart your cycle**
21:00	
22:00	
23:00	**Positive affirmation**
Notes	

Friday | 26 February 2021

6:00	
7:00	
8:00	
9:00	
10:00	
11:00	
12:00	
13:00	
14:00	
15:00	
16:00	
17:00	
18:00	
19:00	
20:00	
21:00	
22:00	
23:00	

Notes

Today's quick wins

Health and nutrition

Today, I am grateful for...

Today's self care

Chart your cycle

Positive affirmation

Saturday | 27 February 2021

6:00	**Today's quick wins**
7:00	
8:00	
9:00	
10:00	
11:00	**Health and nutrition**
12:00	
13:00	
14:00	**Today, I am grateful for...**
15:00	
16:00	
17:00	**Today's self care**
18:00	
19:00	
20:00	**Chart your cycle**
21:00	
22:00	
23:00	**Positive affirmation**
Notes	

Sunday | 28 February 2021

6:00	
7:00	
8:00	
9:00	
10:00	
11:00	
12:00	
13:00	
14:00	
15:00	
16:00	
17:00	
18:00	
19:00	
20:00	
21:00	
22:00	
23:00	

Today's quick wins

Health and nutrition

Today, I am grateful for...

Today's self care

Chart your cycle

Positive affirmation

Notes

February achievements

Be proud of yourself and all that you have achieved this month. Write down your wins, big and small. If you have not achieved everything that you set out to do, that's okay! We learn and grow through our mistakes and experiences. You can use this space to make notes about anything that you have learned.

March 2021

Notes	Monday	Tuesday	Wednesday
	1	2	3
	8	9	10
	15	16	17
	22	23	24
	29	30	31

Thursday	Friday	Saturday	Sunday
4	5	6 ☽	7
11	12	13 ●	14
18	19	20 *Spring equinox*	21 ☾
25	26	27	28 ○
1	2	3	4

March

Worm moon

March goals

Use this space to write your goals for the month ahead, and any steps you can take that will get you to where you want to be.

Monday | 1 March 2021

6:00	**Today's quick wins**
7:00	
8:00	
9:00	
10:00	
11:00	**Health and nutrition**
12:00	
13:00	
14:00	**Today, I am grateful for...**
15:00	
16:00	
17:00	**Today's self care**
18:00	
19:00	
20:00	**Chart your cycle**
21:00	
22:00	
23:00	**Positive affirmation**
Notes	

Tuesday | 2 March 2021

6:00	
7:00	
8:00	
9:00	
10:00	
11:00	
12:00	
13:00	
14:00	
15:00	
16:00	
17:00	
18:00	
19:00	
20:00	
21:00	
22:00	
23:00	

Today's quick wins

Health and nutrition

Today, I am grateful for...

Today's self care

Chart your cycle

Positive affirmation

Notes

Wednesday | 3 March 2021

6:00	**Today's quick wins**
7:00	
8:00	
9:00	
10:00	
11:00	**Health and nutrition**
12:00	
13:00	
14:00	**Today, I am grateful for...**
15:00	
16:00	
17:00	**Today's self care**
18:00	
19:00	
20:00	**Chart your cycle**
21:00	
22:00	
23:00	**Positive affirmation**
Notes	

Thursday | 4 March 2021

6:00	**Today's quick wins**
7:00	
8:00	
9:00	
10:00	
11:00	**Health and nutrition**
12:00	
13:00	
14:00	**Today, I am grateful for...**
15:00	
16:00	
17:00	**Today's self care**
18:00	
19:00	
20:00	**Chart your cycle**
21:00	
22:00	
23:00	**Positive affirmation**
Notes	

Friday | 5 March 2021

6:00	**Today's quick wins**
7:00	
8:00	
9:00	
10:00	
11:00	**Health and nutrition**
12:00	
13:00	
14:00	**Today, I am grateful for...**
15:00	
16:00	
17:00	**Today's self care**
18:00	
19:00	
20:00	**Chart your cycle**
21:00	
22:00	
23:00	**Positive affirmation**
Notes	

Saturday | 6 March 2021

6:00	**Today's quick wins**
7:00	
8:00	
9:00	
10:00	
11:00	**Health and nutrition**
12:00	
13:00	
14:00	**Today, I am grateful for...**
15:00	
16:00	
17:00	**Today's self care**
18:00	
19:00	
20:00	**Chart your cycle**
21:00	
22:00	
23:00	**Positive affirmation**
Notes	

Sunday | 7 March 2021

6:00	**Today's quick wins**
7:00	
8:00	
9:00	
10:00	
11:00	**Health and nutrition**
12:00	
13:00	
14:00	**Today, I am grateful for...**
15:00	
16:00	
17:00	**Today's self care**
18:00	
19:00	
20:00	**Chart your cycle**
21:00	
22:00	
23:00	**Positive affirmation**
Notes	

Monday | 8 March 2021

6:00	
7:00	
8:00	
9:00	
10:00	
11:00	
12:00	
13:00	
14:00	
15:00	
16:00	
17:00	
18:00	
19:00	
20:00	
21:00	
22:00	
23:00	

Today's quick wins

Health and nutrition

Today, I am grateful for...

Today's self care

Chart your cycle

Positive affirmation

Notes

Tuesday | 9 March 2021

6:00	**Today's quick wins**
7:00	
8:00	
9:00	
10:00	
11:00	**Health and nutrition**
12:00	
13:00	
14:00	**Today, I am grateful for...**
15:00	
16:00	
17:00	**Today's self care**
18:00	
19:00	
20:00	**Chart your cycle**
21:00	
22:00	
23:00	**Positive affirmation**
Notes	

Wednesday | 10 March 2021

6:00	
7:00	
8:00	
9:00	
10:00	
11:00	
12:00	
13:00	
14:00	
15:00	
16:00	
17:00	
18:00	
19:00	
20:00	
21:00	
22:00	
23:00	
Notes	

Today's quick wins

Health and nutrition

Today, I am grateful for...

Today's self care

Chart your cycle

Positive affirmation

Thursday | 11 March 2021

6:00	
7:00	
8:00	
9:00	
10:00	
11:00	
12:00	
13:00	
14:00	
15:00	
16:00	
17:00	
18:00	
19:00	
20:00	
21:00	
22:00	
23:00	

Today's quick wins

Health and nutrition

Today, I am grateful for...

Today's self care

Chart your cycle

Positive affirmation

Notes

Friday | 12 March 2021

6:00	
7:00	
8:00	
9:00	
10:00	
11:00	
12:00	
13:00	
14:00	
15:00	
16:00	
17:00	
18:00	
19:00	
20:00	
21:00	
22:00	
23:00	

Notes

Today's quick wins

Health and nutrition

Today, I am grateful for...

Today's self care

Chart your cycle

Positive affirmation

Saturday | 13 March 2021

6:00	
7:00	
8:00	
9:00	
10:00	
11:00	
12:00	
13:00	
14:00	
15:00	
16:00	
17:00	
18:00	
19:00	
20:00	
21:00	
22:00	
23:00	

Today's quick wins

Health and nutrition

Today, I am grateful for...

Today's self care

Chart your cycle

Positive affirmation

Notes

Sunday | 14 March 2021

6:00	**Today's quick wins**
7:00	
8:00	
9:00	
10:00	
11:00	**Health and nutrition**
12:00	
13:00	
14:00	**Today, I am grateful for...**
15:00	
16:00	
17:00	**Today's self care**
18:00	
19:00	
20:00	**Chart your cycle**
21:00	
22:00	
23:00	**Positive affirmation**
Notes	

Monday | 15 March 2021

6:00	
7:00	
8:00	
9:00	
10:00	
11:00	
12:00	
13:00	
14:00	
15:00	
16:00	
17:00	
18:00	
19:00	
20:00	
21:00	
22:00	
23:00	

Today's quick wins

Health and nutrition

Today, I am grateful for...

Today's self care

Chart your cycle

Positive affirmation

Notes

Tuesday | 16 March 2021

6:00	**Today's quick wins**
7:00	
8:00	
9:00	
10:00	
11:00	**Health and nutrition**
12:00	
13:00	
14:00	**Today, I am grateful for...**
15:00	
16:00	
17:00	**Today's self care**
18:00	
19:00	
20:00	**Chart your cycle**
21:00	
22:00	
23:00	**Positive affirmation**
Notes	

Wednesday | 17 March 2021

6:00	
7:00	
8:00	
9:00	
10:00	
11:00	
12:00	
13:00	
14:00	
15:00	
16:00	
17:00	
18:00	
19:00	
20:00	
21:00	
22:00	
23:00	

Notes

Today's quick wins

Health and nutrition

Today, I am grateful for...

Today's self care

Chart your cycle

Positive affirmation

Thursday | 18 March 2021

6:00	
7:00	
8:00	
9:00	
10:00	
11:00	
12:00	
13:00	
14:00	
15:00	
16:00	
17:00	
18:00	
19:00	
20:00	
21:00	
22:00	
23:00	

Today's quick wins

Health and nutrition

Today, I am grateful for...

Today's self care

Chart your cycle

Positive affirmation

Notes

Friday | 19 March 2021

6:00	**Today's quick wins**
7:00	
8:00	
9:00	
10:00	
11:00	**Health and nutrition**
12:00	
13:00	
14:00	**Today, I am grateful for...**
15:00	
16:00	
17:00	**Today's self care**
18:00	
19:00	
20:00	**Chart your cycle**
21:00	
22:00	
23:00	**Positive affirmation**
Notes	

Saturday | 20 March 2021 - *Spring equinox*

6:00	
7:00	
8:00	
9:00	
10:00	
11:00	
12:00	
13:00	
14:00	
15:00	
16:00	
17:00	
18:00	
19:00	
20:00	
21:00	
22:00	
23:00	

Today's quick wins

Health and nutrition

Today, I am grateful for...

Today's self care

Chart your cycle

Positive affirmation

Notes

Sunday | 21 January 2021

6:00	**Today's quick wins**
7:00	
8:00	
9:00	
10:00	
11:00	**Health and nutrition**
12:00	
13:00	
14:00	**Today, I am grateful for...**
15:00	
16:00	
17:00	**Today's self care**
18:00	
19:00	
20:00	**Chart your cycle**
21:00	
22:00	
23:00	**Positive affirmation**
Notes	

Monday | 22 March 2021

6:00	
7:00	
8:00	
9:00	
10:00	
11:00	
12:00	
13:00	
14:00	
15:00	
16:00	
17:00	
18:00	
19:00	
20:00	
21:00	
22:00	
23:00	

Notes

Today's quick wins

Health and nutrition

Today, I am grateful for...

Today's self care

Chart your cycle

Positive affirmation

Tuesday | 23 March 2021

6:00	**Today's quick wins**
7:00	
8:00	
9:00	
10:00	
11:00	**Health and nutrition**
12:00	
13:00	
14:00	**Today, I am grateful for...**
15:00	
16:00	
17:00	**Today's self care**
18:00	
19:00	
20:00	**Chart your cycle**
21:00	
22:00	
23:00	**Positive affirmation**
Notes	

Wednesday | 24 March 2021

6:00	**Today's quick wins**
7:00	
8:00	
9:00	
10:00	
11:00	**Health and nutrition**
12:00	
13:00	
14:00	**Today, I am grateful for...**
15:00	
16:00	
17:00	**Today's self care**
18:00	
19:00	
20:00	**Chart your cycle**
21:00	
22:00	
23:00	**Positive affirmation**
Notes	

Thursday | 25 March 2021

6:00	**Today's quick wins**
7:00	
8:00	
9:00	
10:00	
11:00	**Health and nutrition**
12:00	
13:00	
14:00	**Today, I am grateful for...**
15:00	
16:00	
17:00	**Today's self care**
18:00	
19:00	
20:00	**Chart your cycle**
21:00	
22:00	
23:00	**Positive affirmation**
Notes	

Friday | 26 March 2021

6:00	**Today's quick wins**
7:00	
8:00	
9:00	
10:00	
11:00	**Health and nutrition**
12:00	
13:00	
14:00	**Today, I am grateful for...**
15:00	
16:00	
17:00	**Today's self care**
18:00	
19:00	
20:00	**Chart your cycle**
21:00	
22:00	
23:00	**Positive affirmation**
Notes	

Saturday | 27 March 2021

6:00	
7:00	
8:00	
9:00	
10:00	
11:00	
12:00	
13:00	
14:00	
15:00	
16:00	
17:00	
18:00	
19:00	
20:00	
21:00	
22:00	
23:00	

Today's quick wins

Health and nutrition

Today, I am grateful for...

Today's self care

Chart your cycle

Positive affirmation

Notes

Sunday | 28 March 2021

6:00	**Today's quick wins**
7:00	
8:00	
9:00	
10:00	
11:00	**Health and nutrition**
12:00	
13:00	
14:00	**Today, I am grateful for...**
15:00	
16:00	
17:00	**Today's self care**
18:00	
19:00	
20:00	**Chart your cycle**
21:00	
22:00	
23:00	**Positive affirmation**
Notes	

Monday | 29 March 2021

6:00	**Today's quick wins**
7:00	
8:00	
9:00	
10:00	
11:00	**Health and nutrition**
12:00	
13:00	
14:00	**Today, I am grateful for...**
15:00	
16:00	
17:00	**Today's self care**
18:00	
19:00	
20:00	**Chart your cycle**
21:00	
22:00	
23:00	**Positive affirmation**
Notes	

Tuesday | 30 March 2021

6:00	**Today's quick wins**
7:00	
8:00	
9:00	
10:00	
11:00	**Health and nutrition**
12:00	
13:00	
14:00	**Today, I am grateful for...**
15:00	
16:00	
17:00	**Today's self care**
18:00	
19:00	
20:00	**Chart your cycle**
21:00	
22:00	
23:00	**Positive affirmation**
Notes	

Wednesday | 31 March 2021

6:00	
7:00	
8:00	
9:00	
10:00	
11:00	
12:00	
13:00	
14:00	
15:00	
16:00	
17:00	
18:00	
19:00	
20:00	
21:00	
22:00	
23:00	

Notes

Today's quick wins

Health and nutrition

Today, I am grateful for...

Today's self care

Chart your cycle

Positive affirmation

March achievements

Be proud of yourself and all that you have achieved this month. Write down your wins, big and small. If you have not achieved everything that you set out to do, that's okay! We learn and grow through our mistakes and experiences. You can use this space to make notes about anything that you have learned.

April 2021

Notes	Monday	Tuesday	Wednesday
	29	30	31
	5	6	7
	12 ●	13	14
	19	20 ◖	21
	26	27 ○	28

Thursday	Friday	Saturday	Sunday
1	2	3	4 ◗
8	9	10	11
15	16	17	18
22	23	24	25
29	30	1	2

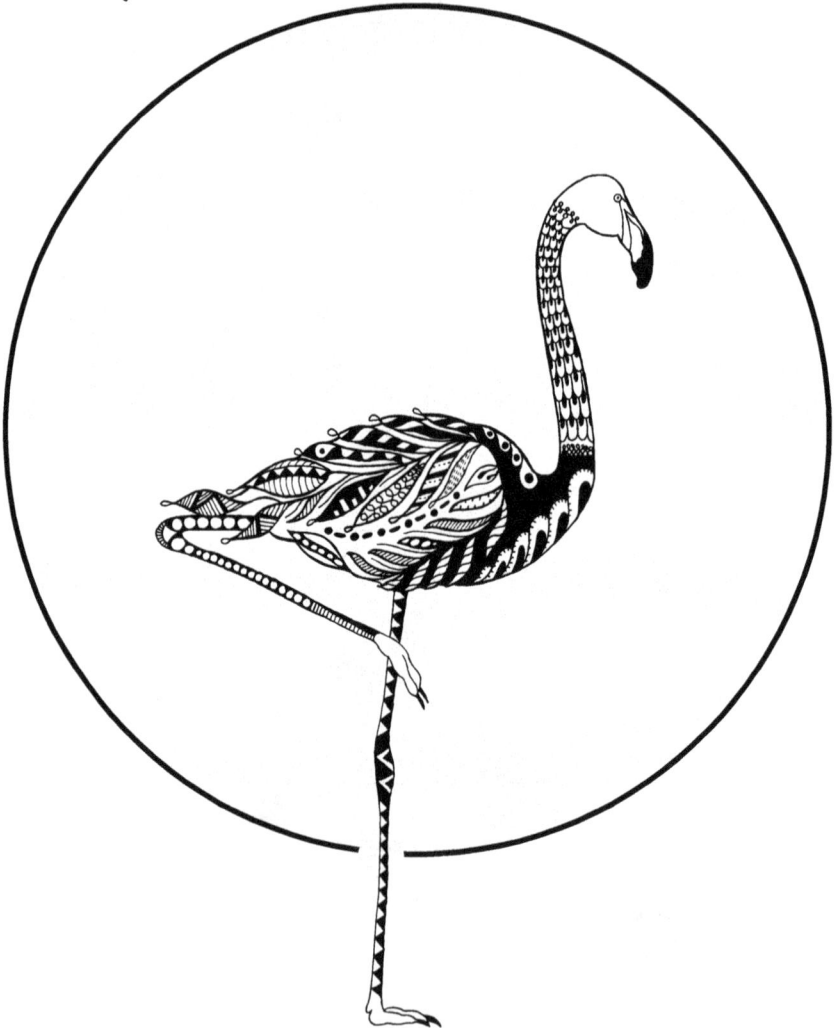

April
Pink moon

April goals

Use this space to write your goals for the month ahead, and any steps you can take that will get you to where you want to be.

Thursday | 1 April 2021

6:00	
7:00	
8:00	
9:00	
10:00	
11:00	
12:00	
13:00	
14:00	
15:00	
16:00	
17:00	
18:00	
19:00	
20:00	
21:00	
22:00	
23:00	

Today's quick wins

Health and nutrition

Today, I am grateful for...

Today's self care

Chart your cycle

Positive affirmation

Notes

Friday | 2 April 2021

6:00	**Today's quick wins**
7:00	
8:00	
9:00	
10:00	
11:00	**Health and nutrition**
12:00	
13:00	
14:00	**Today, I am grateful for...**
15:00	
16:00	
17:00	**Today's self care**
18:00	
19:00	
20:00	**Chart your cycle**
21:00	
22:00	
23:00	**Positive affirmation**
Notes	

Saturday | 3 April 2021

6:00	
7:00	
8:00	
9:00	
10:00	
11:00	
12:00	
13:00	
14:00	
15:00	
16:00	
17:00	
18:00	
19:00	
20:00	
21:00	
22:00	
23:00	

Today's quick wins

Health and nutrition

Today, I am grateful for...

Today's self care

Chart your cycle

Positive affirmation

Notes

Sunday | 4 April 2021

6:00	**Today's quick wins**	
7:00		
8:00		
9:00		
10:00		
11:00	**Health and nutrition**	
12:00		
13:00		
14:00	**Today, I am grateful for…**	
15:00		
16:00		
17:00	**Today's self care**	
18:00		
19:00		
20:00	**Chart your cycle**	
21:00		
22:00		
23:00	**Positive affirmation**	
Notes		

Monday | 5 April 2021

6:00	**Today's quick wins**
7:00	
8:00	
9:00	
10:00	
11:00	**Health and nutrition**
12:00	
13:00	
14:00	**Today, I am grateful for...**
15:00	
16:00	
17:00	**Today's self care**
18:00	
19:00	
20:00	**Chart your cycle**
21:00	
22:00	
23:00	**Positive affirmation**
Notes	

Tuesday | 6 April 2021

6:00	**Today's quick wins**
7:00	
8:00	
9:00	
10:00	
11:00	**Health and nutrition**
12:00	
13:00	
14:00	**Today, I am grateful for...**
15:00	
16:00	
17:00	**Today's self care**
18:00	
19:00	
20:00	**Chart your cycle**
21:00	
22:00	
23:00	**Positive affirmation**
Notes	

Wednesday | 7 April 2021

6:00	
7:00	
8:00	
9:00	
10:00	
11:00	
12:00	
13:00	
14:00	
15:00	
16:00	
17:00	
18:00	
19:00	
20:00	
21:00	
22:00	
23:00	

Today's quick wins

Health and nutrition

Today, I am grateful for...

Today's self care

Chart your cycle

Positive affirmation

Notes

Thursday | 8 April 2021

6:00	
7:00	
8:00	
9:00	
10:00	
11:00	
12:00	
13:00	
14:00	
15:00	
16:00	
17:00	
18:00	
19:00	
20:00	
21:00	
22:00	
23:00	

Today's quick wins

Health and nutrition

Today, I am grateful for...

Today's self care

Chart your cycle

Positive affirmation

Notes

Friday | 9 April 2021

6:00	**Today's quick wins**
7:00	
8:00	
9:00	
10:00	
11:00	**Health and nutrition**
12:00	
13:00	
14:00	**Today, I am grateful for...**
15:00	
16:00	
17:00	**Today's self care**
18:00	
19:00	
20:00	**Chart your cycle**
21:00	
22:00	
23:00	**Positive affirmation**
Notes	

Saturday | 10 April 2021

6:00	**Today's quick wins**
7:00	
8:00	
9:00	
10:00	
11:00	**Health and nutrition**
12:00	
13:00	
14:00	**Today, I am grateful for...**
15:00	
16:00	
17:00	**Today's self care**
18:00	
19:00	
20:00	**Chart your cycle**
21:00	
22:00	
23:00	**Positive affirmation**
Notes	

Sunday | 11 April 2021

6:00	**Today's quick wins**
7:00	
8:00	
9:00	
10:00	
11:00	**Health and nutrition**
12:00	
13:00	
14:00	**Today, I am grateful for...**
15:00	
16:00	
17:00	**Today's self care**
18:00	
19:00	
20:00	**Chart your cycle**
21:00	
22:00	
23:00	**Positive affirmation**
Notes	

Monday | 12 April 2021

6:00	**Today's quick wins**
7:00	
8:00	
9:00	
10:00	
11:00	**Health and nutrition**
12:00	
13:00	
14:00	**Today, I am grateful for...**
15:00	
16:00	
17:00	**Today's self care**
18:00	
19:00	
20:00	**Chart your cycle**
21:00	
22:00	
23:00	**Positive affirmation**
Notes	

Tuesday | 13 April 2021

6:00	
7:00	
8:00	
9:00	
10:00	
11:00	
12:00	
13:00	
14:00	
15:00	
16:00	
17:00	
18:00	
19:00	
20:00	
21:00	
22:00	
23:00	

Notes

Today's quick wins

Health and nutrition

Today, I am grateful for...

Today's self care

Chart your cycle

Positive affirmation

Wednesday | 14 April 2021

6:00	**Today's quick wins**
7:00	
8:00	
9:00	
10:00	
11:00	**Health and nutrition**
12:00	
13:00	
14:00	**Today, I am grateful for...**
15:00	
16:00	
17:00	**Today's self care**
18:00	
19:00	
20:00	**Chart your cycle**
21:00	
22:00	
23:00	**Positive affirmation**
Notes	

Thursday | 15 April 2021

6:00		**Today's quick wins**
7:00		
8:00		
9:00		
10:00		
11:00		**Health and nutrition**
12:00		
13:00		
14:00		**Today, I am grateful for...**
15:00		
16:00		
17:00		**Today's self care**
18:00		
19:00		
20:00		**Chart your cycle**
21:00		
22:00		
23:00		**Positive affirmation**
Notes		

Friday | 16 April 2021

6:00	**Today's quick wins**
7:00	
8:00	
9:00	
10:00	
11:00	**Health and nutrition**
12:00	
13:00	
14:00	**Today, I am grateful for...**
15:00	
16:00	
17:00	**Today's self care**
18:00	
19:00	
20:00	**Chart your cycle**
21:00	
22:00	
23:00	**Positive affirmation**
Notes	

Saturday | 17 April 2021

6:00	**Today's quick wins**
7:00	
8:00	
9:00	
10:00	
11:00	**Health and nutrition**
12:00	
13:00	
14:00	**Today, I am grateful for...**
15:00	
16:00	
17:00	**Today's self care**
18:00	
19:00	
20:00	**Chart your cycle**
21:00	
22:00	
23:00	**Positive affirmation**
Notes	

Sunday | 18 April 2021

6:00	**Today's quick wins**
7:00	
8:00	
9:00	
10:00	
11:00	**Health and nutrition**
12:00	
13:00	
14:00	**Today, I am grateful for...**
15:00	
16:00	
17:00	**Today's self care**
18:00	
19:00	
20:00	**Chart your cycle**
21:00	
22:00	
23:00	**Positive affirmation**
Notes	

Monday | 19 April 2021

6:00	
7:00	
8:00	
9:00	
10:00	
11:00	
12:00	
13:00	
14:00	
15:00	
16:00	
17:00	
18:00	
19:00	
20:00	
21:00	
22:00	
23:00	

Notes

Today's quick wins

Health and nutrition

Today, I am grateful for...

Today's self care

Chart your cycle

Positive affirmation

Tuesday | 20 April 2021

6:00	**Today's quick wins**
7:00	
8:00	
9:00	
10:00	
11:00	**Health and nutrition**
12:00	
13:00	
14:00	**Today, I am grateful for...**
15:00	
16:00	
17:00	**Today's self care**
18:00	
19:00	
20:00	**Chart your cycle**
21:00	
22:00	
23:00	**Positive affirmation**
Notes	

Wednesday | 21 April 2021

6:00	**Today's quick wins**
7:00	
8:00	
9:00	
10:00	
11:00	**Health and nutrition**
12:00	
13:00	
14:00	**Today, I am grateful for...**
15:00	
16:00	
17:00	**Today's self care**
18:00	
19:00	
20:00	**Chart your cycle**
21:00	
22:00	
23:00	**Positive affirmation**
Notes	

Thursday | 22 April 2021

6:00	**Today's quick wins**
7:00	
8:00	
9:00	
10:00	
11:00	**Health and nutrition**
12:00	
13:00	
14:00	**Today, I am grateful for...**
15:00	
16:00	
17:00	**Today's self care**
18:00	
19:00	
20:00	**Chart your cycle**
21:00	
22:00	
23:00	**Positive affirmation**
Notes	

Friday | 23 April 2021

6:00	
7:00	
8:00	
9:00	
10:00	
11:00	
12:00	
13:00	
14:00	
15:00	
16:00	
17:00	
18:00	
19:00	
20:00	
21:00	
22:00	
23:00	

Notes

Today's quick wins

Health and nutrition

Today, I am grateful for...

Today's self care

Chart your cycle

Positive affirmation

Saturday | 24 April 2021

6:00	**Today's quick wins**
7:00	
8:00	
9:00	
10:00	
11:00	**Health and nutrition**
12:00	
13:00	
14:00	**Today, I am grateful for...**
15:00	
16:00	
17:00	**Today's self care**
18:00	
19:00	
20:00	**Chart your cycle**
21:00	
22:00	
23:00	**Positive affirmation**
Notes	

Sunday | 25 April 2021

6:00	**Today's quick wins**
7:00	
8:00	
9:00	
10:00	
11:00	**Health and nutrition**
12:00	
13:00	
14:00	**Today, I am grateful for...**
15:00	
16:00	
17:00	**Today's self care**
18:00	
19:00	
20:00	**Chart your cycle**
21:00	
22:00	
23:00	**Positive affirmation**
Notes	

Monday | 26 April 2021

6:00	**Today's quick wins**
7:00	
8:00	
9:00	
10:00	
11:00	**Health and nutrition**
12:00	
13:00	
14:00	**Today, I am grateful for...**
15:00	
16:00	
17:00	**Today's self care**
18:00	
19:00	
20:00	**Chart your cycle**
21:00	
22:00	
23:00	**Positive affirmation**
Notes	

Tuesday | 27 April 2021

6:00		**Today's quick wins**
7:00		
8:00		
9:00		
10:00		
11:00		**Health and nutrition**
12:00		
13:00		
14:00		**Today, I am grateful for...**
15:00		
16:00		
17:00		**Today's self care**
18:00		
19:00		
20:00		**Chart your cycle**
21:00		
22:00		
23:00		**Positive affirmation**
Notes		

Wednesday | 28 April 2021

6:00	**Today's quick wins**
7:00	
8:00	
9:00	
10:00	
11:00	**Health and nutrition**
12:00	
13:00	
14:00	**Today, I am grateful for...**
15:00	
16:00	
17:00	**Today's self care**
18:00	
19:00	
20:00	**Chart your cycle**
21:00	
22:00	
23:00	**Positive affirmation**
Notes	

Thursday | 29 April 2021

6:00	**Today's quick wins**
7:00	
8:00	
9:00	
10:00	
11:00	**Health and nutrition**
12:00	
13:00	
14:00	**Today, I am grateful for...**
15:00	
16:00	
17:00	**Today's self care**
18:00	
19:00	
20:00	**Chart your cycle**
21:00	
22:00	
23:00	**Positive affirmation**
Notes	

Friday | 30 April 2021

6:00	**Today's quick wins**
7:00	
8:00	
9:00	
10:00	
11:00	**Health and nutrition**
12:00	
13:00	
14:00	**Today, I am grateful for...**
15:00	
16:00	
17:00	**Today's self care**
18:00	
19:00	
20:00	**Chart your cycle**
21:00	
22:00	
23:00	**Positive affirmation**
Notes	

April achievements

Be proud of yourself and all that you have achieved this month. Write down your wins, big and small. If you have not achieved everything that you set out to do, that's okay! We learn and grow through our mistakes and experiences. You can use this space to make notes about anything that you have learned.

'You must become the producer, director and actor in the unfolding story of your life.'

— Dr Wayne Dyer

May 2021

Notes	Monday	Tuesday	Wednesday
	26	27	28
	3 ◗	4	5
	10	11 ●	12
	17	18	19 ◖
	24	25	26 ○

Thursday	Friday	Saturday	Sunday
29	30	1	2
6	7	8	9
13	14	15	16
20	21	22	23
27	28	29	30
			31 (Monday)

May

Flower moon

May goals

Use this space to write your goals for the month ahead, and any steps you can take that will get you to where you want to be.

Saturday | 1 May 2021

6:00	
7:00	
8:00	
9:00	
10:00	
11:00	
12:00	
13:00	
14:00	
15:00	
16:00	
17:00	
18:00	
19:00	
20:00	
21:00	
22:00	
23:00	

Today's quick wins

Health and nutrition

Today, I am grateful for...

Today's self care

Chart your cycle

Positive affirmation

Notes

Sunday | 2 May 2021

6:00	**Today's quick wins**
7:00	
8:00	
9:00	
10:00	
11:00	**Health and nutrition**
12:00	
13:00	
14:00	**Today, I am grateful for...**
15:00	
16:00	
17:00	**Today's self care**
18:00	
19:00	
20:00	**Chart your cycle**
21:00	
22:00	
23:00	**Positive affirmation**
Notes	

Monday | 3 May 2021

6:00	**Today's quick wins**
7:00	
8:00	
9:00	
10:00	
11:00	**Health and nutrition**
12:00	
13:00	
14:00	**Today, I am grateful for...**
15:00	
16:00	
17:00	**Today's self care**
18:00	
19:00	
20:00	**Chart your cycle**
21:00	
22:00	
23:00	**Positive affirmation**
Notes	

Tuesday | 4 May 2021

6:00	**Today's quick wins**
7:00	
8:00	
9:00	
10:00	
11:00	**Health and nutrition**
12:00	
13:00	
14:00	**Today, I am grateful for...**
15:00	
16:00	
17:00	**Today's self care**
18:00	
19:00	
20:00	**Chart your cycle**
21:00	
22:00	
23:00	**Positive affirmation**
Notes	

Wednesday | 5 May 2021

6:00	**Today's quick wins**
7:00	
8:00	
9:00	
10:00	
11:00	**Health and nutrition**
12:00	
13:00	
14:00	**Today, I am grateful for...**
15:00	
16:00	
17:00	**Today's self care**
18:00	
19:00	
20:00	**Chart your cycle**
21:00	
22:00	
23:00	**Positive affirmation**
Notes	

Thursday | 6 May 2021

6:00	
7:00	
8:00	
9:00	
10:00	
11:00	
12:00	
13:00	
14:00	
15:00	
16:00	
17:00	
18:00	
19:00	
20:00	
21:00	
22:00	
23:00	

Today's quick wins

Health and nutrition

Today, I am grateful for...

Today's self care

Chart your cycle

Positive affirmation

Notes

Friday | 7 May 2021

6:00	
7:00	
8:00	
9:00	
10:00	
11:00	
12:00	
13:00	
14:00	
15:00	
16:00	
17:00	
18:00	
19:00	
20:00	
21:00	
22:00	
23:00	

Notes

Today's quick wins

Health and nutrition

Today, I am grateful for...

Today's self care

Chart your cycle

Positive affirmation

Saturday | 8 May 2021

6:00	**Today's quick wins**
7:00	
8:00	
9:00	
10:00	
11:00	**Health and nutrition**
12:00	
13:00	
14:00	**Today, I am grateful for...**
15:00	
16:00	
17:00	**Today's self care**
18:00	
19:00	
20:00	**Chart your cycle**
21:00	
22:00	
23:00	**Positive affirmation**
Notes	

Sunday | 9 May 2021

6:00	
7:00	
8:00	
9:00	
10:00	
11:00	
12:00	
13:00	
14:00	
15:00	
16:00	
17:00	
18:00	
19:00	
20:00	
21:00	
22:00	
23:00	

Today's quick wins

Health and nutrition

Today, I am grateful for...

Today's self care

Chart your cycle

Positive affirmation

Notes

Monday | 10 May 2021

6:00		**Today's quick wins**
7:00		
8:00		
9:00		
10:00		
11:00		**Health and nutrition**
12:00		
13:00		
14:00		**Today, I am grateful for...**
15:00		
16:00		
17:00		**Today's self care**
18:00		
19:00		
20:00		**Chart your cycle**
21:00		
22:00		
23:00		**Positive affirmation**
Notes		

Tuesday | 11 May 2021

6:00	
7:00	
8:00	
9:00	
10:00	
11:00	
12:00	
13:00	
14:00	
15:00	
16:00	
17:00	
18:00	
19:00	
20:00	
21:00	
22:00	
23:00	

Today's quick wins

Health and nutrition

Today, I am grateful for...

Today's self care

Chart your cycle

Positive affirmation

Notes

Wednesday | 12 May 2021

6:00	**Today's quick wins**
7:00	
8:00	
9:00	
10:00	
11:00	**Health and nutrition**
12:00	
13:00	
14:00	**Today, I am grateful for...**
15:00	
16:00	
17:00	**Today's self care**
18:00	
19:00	
20:00	**Chart your cycle**
21:00	
22:00	
23:00	**Positive affirmation**
Notes	

Thursday | 13 May 2021

6:00	
7:00	
8:00	
9:00	
10:00	
11:00	
12:00	
13:00	
14:00	
15:00	
16:00	
17:00	
18:00	
19:00	
20:00	
21:00	
22:00	
23:00	

Today's quick wins

Health and nutrition

Today, I am grateful for...

Today's self care

Chart your cycle

Positive affirmation

Notes

Friday | 14 May 2021

6:00	**Today's quick wins**
7:00	
8:00	
9:00	
10:00	
11:00	**Health and nutrition**
12:00	
13:00	
14:00	**Today, I am grateful for...**
15:00	
16:00	
17:00	**Today's self care**
18:00	
19:00	
20:00	**Chart your cycle**
21:00	
22:00	
23:00	**Positive affirmation**
Notes	

Saturday | 15 May 2021

6:00	
7:00	
8:00	
9:00	
10:00	
11:00	
12:00	
13:00	
14:00	
15:00	
16:00	
17:00	
18:00	
19:00	
20:00	
21:00	
22:00	
23:00	

Today's quick wins

Health and nutrition

Today, I am grateful for...

Today's self care

Chart your cycle

Positive affirmation

Notes

Sunday | 16 May 2021

6:00	**Today's quick wins**
7:00	
8:00	
9:00	
10:00	
11:00	**Health and nutrition**
12:00	
13:00	
14:00	**Today, I am grateful for...**
15:00	
16:00	
17:00	**Today's self care**
18:00	
19:00	
20:00	**Chart your cycle**
21:00	
22:00	
23:00	**Positive affirmation**
Notes	

Monday | 17 May 2021

6:00	**Today's quick wins**
7:00	
8:00	
9:00	
10:00	
11:00	**Health and nutrition**
12:00	
13:00	
14:00	**Today, I am grateful for...**
15:00	
16:00	
17:00	**Today's self care**
18:00	
19:00	
20:00	**Chart your cycle**
21:00	
22:00	
23:00	**Positive affirmation**
Notes	

Tuesday | 18 May 2021

6:00	**Today's quick wins**
7:00	
8:00	
9:00	
10:00	
11:00	**Health and nutrition**
12:00	
13:00	
14:00	**Today, I am grateful for...**
15:00	
16:00	
17:00	**Today's self care**
18:00	
19:00	
20:00	**Chart your cycle**
21:00	
22:00	
23:00	**Positive affirmation**
Notes	

Wednesday | 19 May 2021

6:00	
7:00	
8:00	
9:00	
10:00	
11:00	
12:00	
13:00	
14:00	
15:00	
16:00	
17:00	
18:00	
19:00	
20:00	
21:00	
22:00	
23:00	

Today's quick wins

Health and nutrition

Today, I am grateful for...

Today's self care

Chart your cycle

Positive affirmation

Notes

Thursday | 20 May 2021

6:00	
7:00	
8:00	
9:00	
10:00	
11:00	
12:00	
13:00	
14:00	
15:00	
16:00	
17:00	
18:00	
19:00	
20:00	
21:00	
22:00	
23:00	

Today's quick wins

Health and nutrition

Today, I am grateful for...

Today's self care

Chart your cycle

Positive affirmation

Notes

Friday | 21 May 2021

6:00	
7:00	
8:00	
9:00	
10:00	
11:00	
12:00	
13:00	
14:00	
15:00	
16:00	
17:00	
18:00	
19:00	
20:00	
21:00	
22:00	
23:00	

Notes

Today's quick wins

Health and nutrition

Today, I am grateful for...

Today's self care

Chart your cycle

Positive affirmation

Saturday | 22 May 2021

6:00	
7:00	
8:00	
9:00	
10:00	
11:00	
12:00	
13:00	
14:00	
15:00	
16:00	
17:00	
18:00	
19:00	
20:00	
21:00	
22:00	
23:00	

Today's quick wins

Health and nutrition

Today, I am grateful for...

Today's self care

Chart your cycle

Positive affirmation

Notes

Sunday | 23 May 2021

6:00	**Today's quick wins**
7:00	
8:00	
9:00	
10:00	
11:00	**Health and nutrition**
12:00	
13:00	
14:00	**Today, I am grateful for...**
15:00	
16:00	
17:00	**Today's self care**
18:00	
19:00	
20:00	**Chart your cycle**
21:00	
22:00	
23:00	**Positive affirmation**
Notes	

Monday | 24 May 2021

6:00	**Today's quick wins**
7:00	
8:00	
9:00	
10:00	
11:00	**Health and nutrition**
12:00	
13:00	
14:00	**Today, I am grateful for...**
15:00	
16:00	
17:00	**Today's self care**
18:00	
19:00	
20:00	**Chart your cycle**
21:00	
22:00	
23:00	**Positive affirmation**
Notes	

Tuesday | 25 May 2021

6:00	
7:00	
8:00	
9:00	
10:00	
11:00	
12:00	
13:00	
14:00	
15:00	
16:00	
17:00	
18:00	
19:00	
20:00	
21:00	
22:00	
23:00	

Today's quick wins

Health and nutrition

Today, I am grateful for...

Today's self care

Chart your cycle

Positive affirmation

Notes

Wednesday | 26 May 2021

6:00	**Today's quick wins**
7:00	
8:00	
9:00	
10:00	
11:00	**Health and nutrition**
12:00	
13:00	
14:00	**Today, I am grateful for...**
15:00	
16:00	
17:00	**Today's self care**
18:00	
19:00	
20:00	**Chart your cycle**
21:00	
22:00	
23:00	**Positive affirmation**
Notes	

Thursday | 27 May 2021

6:00	**Today's quick wins**
7:00	
8:00	
9:00	
10:00	
11:00	**Health and nutrition**
12:00	
13:00	
14:00	**Today, I am grateful for...**
15:00	
16:00	
17:00	**Today's self care**
18:00	
19:00	
20:00	**Chart your cycle**
21:00	
22:00	
23:00	**Positive affirmation**
Notes	

Friday | 28 May 2021

6:00	**Today's quick wins**
7:00	
8:00	
9:00	
10:00	
11:00	**Health and nutrition**
12:00	
13:00	
14:00	**Today, I am grateful for...**
15:00	
16:00	
17:00	**Today's self care**
18:00	
19:00	
20:00	**Chart your cycle**
21:00	
22:00	
23:00	**Positive affirmation**
Notes	

Saturday | 29 May 2021

6:00	**Today's quick wins**
7:00	
8:00	
9:00	
10:00	
11:00	**Health and nutrition**
12:00	
13:00	
14:00	**Today, I am grateful for...**
15:00	
16:00	
17:00	**Today's self care**
18:00	
19:00	
20:00	**Chart your cycle**
21:00	
22:00	
23:00	**Positive affirmation**
Notes	

Sunday | 30 May 2021

6:00	**Today's quick wins**
7:00	
8:00	
9:00	
10:00	
11:00	**Health and nutrition**
12:00	
13:00	
14:00	**Today, I am grateful for...**
15:00	
16:00	
17:00	**Today's self care**
18:00	
19:00	
20:00	**Chart your cycle**
21:00	
22:00	
23:00	**Positive affirmation**
Notes	

Monday | 31 May 2021

6:00	
7:00	
8:00	
9:00	
10:00	
11:00	
12:00	
13:00	
14:00	
15:00	
16:00	
17:00	
18:00	
19:00	
20:00	
21:00	
22:00	
23:00	

Notes

Today's quick wins

Health and nutrition

Today, I am grateful for...

Today's self care

Chart your cycle

Positive affirmation

May achievements

Be proud of yourself and all that you have achieved this month. Write down your wins, big and small. If you have not achieved everything that you set out to do, that's okay! We learn and grow through our mistakes and experiences. You can use this space to make notes about anything that you have learned.

June 2021

Notes	Monday	Tuesday	Wednesday
	31	1	2 ◗
	7	8	9
	14	15	16
	21 *Summer solstice*	22	23
	28	29	30

Thursday	Friday	Saturday	Sunday
3	4	5	6
10 ●	11	12	13
17	18 ◗	19	20
24 ○	25	26	27
1	2	3	4

June

Strawberry
moon

June goals

Use this space to write your goals for the month ahead, and any steps you can take that will get you to where you want to be.

Tuesday | 1 June 2021

6:00	**Today's quick wins**
7:00	
8:00	
9:00	
10:00	
11:00	**Health and nutrition**
12:00	
13:00	
14:00	**Today, I am grateful for...**
15:00	
16:00	
17:00	**Today's self care**
18:00	
19:00	
20:00	**Chart your cycle**
21:00	
22:00	
23:00	**Positive affirmation**
Notes	

Wednesday | 2 June 2021

6:00	**Today's quick wins**
7:00	
8:00	
9:00	
10:00	
11:00	**Health and nutrition**
12:00	
13:00	
14:00	**Today, I am grateful for...**
15:00	
16:00	
17:00	**Today's self care**
18:00	
19:00	
20:00	**Chart your cycle**
21:00	
22:00	
23:00	**Positive affirmation**
Notes	

Thursday | 3 June 2021

6:00	**Today's quick wins**
7:00	
8:00	
9:00	
10:00	
11:00	**Health and nutrition**
12:00	
13:00	
14:00	**Today, I am grateful for...**
15:00	
16:00	
17:00	**Today's self care**
18:00	
19:00	
20:00	**Chart your cycle**
21:00	
22:00	
23:00	**Positive affirmation**
Notes	

Friday | 4 June 2021

6:00	
7:00	
8:00	
9:00	
10:00	
11:00	
12:00	
13:00	
14:00	
15:00	
16:00	
17:00	
18:00	
19:00	
20:00	
21:00	
22:00	
23:00	

Today's quick wins

Health and nutrition

Today, I am grateful for...

Today's self care

Chart your cycle

Positive affirmation

Notes

Saturday | 5 June 2021

6:00	
7:00	
8:00	
9:00	
10:00	
11:00	
12:00	
13:00	
14:00	
15:00	
16:00	
17:00	
18:00	
19:00	
20:00	
21:00	
22:00	
23:00	

Today's quick wins

Health and nutrition

Today, I am grateful for...

Today's self care

Chart your cycle

Positive affirmation

Notes

Sunday | 6 June 2021

6:00	**Today's quick wins**
7:00	
8:00	
9:00	
10:00	
11:00	**Health and nutrition**
12:00	
13:00	
14:00	**Today, I am grateful for...**
15:00	
16:00	
17:00	**Today's self care**
18:00	
19:00	
20:00	**Chart your cycle**
21:00	
22:00	
23:00	**Positive affirmation**
Notes	

Monday | 7 June 2021

6:00	**Today's quick wins**
7:00	
8:00	
9:00	
10:00	
11:00	**Health and nutrition**
12:00	
13:00	
14:00	**Today, I am grateful for...**
15:00	
16:00	
17:00	**Today's self care**
18:00	
19:00	
20:00	**Chart your cycle**
21:00	
22:00	
23:00	**Positive affirmation**
Notes	

Tuesday | 8 June 2021

6:00	**Today's quick wins**
7:00	
8:00	
9:00	
10:00	
11:00	**Health and nutrition**
12:00	
13:00	
14:00	**Today, I am grateful for...**
15:00	
16:00	
17:00	**Today's self care**
18:00	
19:00	
20:00	**Chart your cycle**
21:00	
22:00	
23:00	**Positive affirmation**
Notes	

Wednesday | 9 June 2021

6:00	
7:00	
8:00	
9:00	
10:00	
11:00	
12:00	
13:00	
14:00	
15:00	
16:00	
17:00	
18:00	
19:00	
20:00	
21:00	
22:00	
23:00	

Today's quick wins

Health and nutrition

Today, I am grateful for...

Today's self care

Chart your cycle

Positive affirmation

Notes

Thursday | 10 June 2021

6:00	**Today's quick wins**
7:00	
8:00	
9:00	
10:00	
11:00	**Health and nutrition**
12:00	
13:00	
14:00	**Today, I am grateful for...**
15:00	
16:00	
17:00	**Today's self care**
18:00	
19:00	
20:00	**Chart your cycle**
21:00	
22:00	
23:00	**Positive affirmation**
Notes	

Friday | 11 June 2021

6:00	
7:00	
8:00	
9:00	
10:00	
11:00	
12:00	
13:00	
14:00	
15:00	
16:00	
17:00	
18:00	
19:00	
20:00	
21:00	
22:00	
23:00	

Today's quick wins

Health and nutrition

Today, I am grateful for...

Today's self care

Chart your cycle

Positive affirmation

Notes

Saturday | 12 June 2021

6:00	**Today's quick wins**
7:00	
8:00	
9:00	
10:00	
11:00	**Health and nutrition**
12:00	
13:00	
14:00	**Today, I am grateful for...**
15:00	
16:00	
17:00	**Today's self care**
18:00	
19:00	
20:00	**Chart your cycle**
21:00	
22:00	
23:00	**Positive affirmation**
Notes	

Sunday | 13 June 2021

6:00	
7:00	
8:00	
9:00	
10:00	
11:00	
12:00	
13:00	
14:00	
15:00	
16:00	
17:00	
18:00	
19:00	
20:00	
21:00	
22:00	
23:00	

Today's quick wins

Health and nutrition

Today, I am grateful for...

Today's self care

Chart your cycle

Positive affirmation

Notes

Monday | 14 June 2021

6:00	**Today's quick wins**
7:00	
8:00	
9:00	
10:00	
11:00	**Health and nutrition**
12:00	
13:00	
14:00	**Today, I am grateful for...**
15:00	
16:00	
17:00	**Today's self care**
18:00	
19:00	
20:00	**Chart your cycle**
21:00	
22:00	
23:00	**Positive affirmation**
Notes	

Tuesday | 15 June 2021

6:00	**Today's quick wins**
7:00	
8:00	
9:00	
10:00	
11:00	**Health and nutrition**
12:00	
13:00	
14:00	**Today, I am grateful for...**
15:00	
16:00	
17:00	**Today's self care**
18:00	
19:00	
20:00	**Chart your cycle**
21:00	
22:00	
23:00	**Positive affirmation**
Notes	

Wednesday | 16 June 2021

6:00	**Today's quick wins**
7:00	
8:00	
9:00	
10:00	
11:00	**Health and nutrition**
12:00	
13:00	
14:00	**Today, I am grateful for...**
15:00	
16:00	
17:00	**Today's self care**
18:00	
19:00	
20:00	**Chart your cycle**
21:00	
22:00	
23:00	**Positive affirmation**
Notes	

Thursday | 17 June 2021

6:00	**Today's quick wins**
7:00	
8:00	
9:00	
10:00	
11:00	**Health and nutrition**
12:00	
13:00	
14:00	**Today, I am grateful for...**
15:00	
16:00	
17:00	**Today's self care**
18:00	
19:00	
20:00	**Chart your cycle**
21:00	
22:00	
23:00	**Positive affirmation**
Notes	

Friday | 18 June 2021

6:00	**Today's quick wins**
7:00	
8:00	
9:00	
10:00	
11:00	**Health and nutrition**
12:00	
13:00	
14:00	**Today, I am grateful for...**
15:00	
16:00	
17:00	**Today's self care**
18:00	
19:00	
20:00	**Chart your cycle**
21:00	
22:00	
23:00	**Positive affirmation**
Notes	

Saturday | 19 June 2021

6:00	
7:00	
8:00	
9:00	
10:00	
11:00	
12:00	
13:00	
14:00	
15:00	
16:00	
17:00	
18:00	
19:00	
20:00	
21:00	
22:00	
23:00	

Today's quick wins

Health and nutrition

Today, I am grateful for...

Today's self care

Chart your cycle

Positive affirmation

Notes

Sunday | 20 June 2021

6:00	**Today's quick wins**
7:00	
8:00	
9:00	
10:00	
11:00	**Health and nutrition**
12:00	
13:00	
14:00	**Today, I am grateful for...**
15:00	
16:00	
17:00	**Today's self care**
18:00	
19:00	
20:00	**Chart your cycle**
21:00	
22:00	
23:00	**Positive affirmation**
Notes	

Monday | 21 June 2021 - *Summer solstice*

6:00	**Today's quick wins**
7:00	
8:00	
9:00	
10:00	
11:00	**Health and nutrition**
12:00	
13:00	
14:00	**Today, I am grateful for...**
15:00	
16:00	
17:00	**Today's self care**
18:00	
19:00	
20:00	**Chart your cycle**
21:00	
22:00	
23:00	**Positive affirmation**
Notes	

Tuesday | 22 June 2021

6:00	**Today's quick wins**
7:00	
8:00	
9:00	
10:00	
11:00	**Health and nutrition**
12:00	
13:00	
14:00	**Today, I am grateful for...**
15:00	
16:00	
17:00	**Today's self care**
18:00	
19:00	
20:00	**Chart your cycle**
21:00	
22:00	
23:00	**Positive affirmation**
Notes	

Wednesday | 23 June 2021

6:00	**Today's quick wins**
7:00	
8:00	
9:00	
10:00	
11:00	**Health and nutrition**
12:00	
13:00	
14:00	**Today, I am grateful for...**
15:00	
16:00	
17:00	**Today's self care**
18:00	
19:00	
20:00	**Chart your cycle**
21:00	
22:00	
23:00	**Positive affirmation**
Notes	

Thursday | 24 June 2021

6:00	**Today's quick wins**
7:00	
8:00	
9:00	
10:00	
11:00	**Health and nutrition**
12:00	
13:00	
14:00	**Today, I am grateful for...**
15:00	
16:00	
17:00	**Today's self care**
18:00	
19:00	
20:00	**Chart your cycle**
21:00	
22:00	
23:00	**Positive affirmation**
Notes	

Friday | 25 June 2021

6:00	
7:00	
8:00	
9:00	
10:00	
11:00	
12:00	
13:00	
14:00	
15:00	
16:00	
17:00	
18:00	
19:00	
20:00	
21:00	
22:00	
23:00	

Today's quick wins

Health and nutrition

Today, I am grateful for...

Today's self care

Chart your cycle

Positive affirmation

Notes

Saturday | 26 June 2021

6:00	
7:00	
8:00	
9:00	
10:00	
11:00	
12:00	
13:00	
14:00	
15:00	
16:00	
17:00	
18:00	
19:00	
20:00	
21:00	
22:00	
23:00	

Today's quick wins

Health and nutrition

Today, I am grateful for...

Today's self care

Chart your cycle

Positive affirmation

Notes

Sunday | 27 June 2021

6:00	**Today's quick wins**
7:00	
8:00	
9:00	
10:00	
11:00	**Health and nutrition**
12:00	
13:00	
14:00	**Today, I am grateful for...**
15:00	
16:00	
17:00	**Today's self care**
18:00	
19:00	
20:00	**Chart your cycle**
21:00	
22:00	
23:00	**Positive affirmation**

Notes

Monday | 28 June 2021

6:00	**Today's quick wins**
7:00	
8:00	
9:00	
10:00	
11:00	**Health and nutrition**
12:00	
13:00	
14:00	**Today, I am grateful for...**
15:00	
16:00	
17:00	**Today's self care**
18:00	
19:00	
20:00	**Chart your cycle**
21:00	
22:00	
23:00	**Positive affirmation**
Notes	

Tuesday | 29 June 2021

6:00	**Today's quick wins**
7:00	
8:00	
9:00	
10:00	
11:00	**Health and nutrition**
12:00	
13:00	
14:00	**Today, I am grateful for...**
15:00	
16:00	
17:00	**Today's self care**
18:00	
19:00	
20:00	**Chart your cycle**
21:00	
22:00	
23:00	**Positive affirmation**
Notes	

Wednesday | 30 June 2021

6:00	
7:00	
8:00	
9:00	
10:00	
11:00	
12:00	
13:00	
14:00	
15:00	
16:00	
17:00	
18:00	
19:00	
20:00	
21:00	
22:00	
23:00	

Notes

Today's quick wins

Health and nutrition

Today, I am grateful for...

Today's self care

Chart your cycle

Positive affirmation

June achievements

Be proud of yourself and all that you have achieved this month. Write down your wins, big and small. If you have not achieved everything that you set out to do, that's okay! We learn and grow through our mistakes and experiences. You can use this space to make notes about anything that you have learned.

To be empowered — to be free.
To be unlimited. To be creative.
To be genius. To be divine — that
is who you are.... Once you feel
this way, memorize this feeling ;
remember this feeling.
This is who you really are.'

— Joe Dispenza

July 2021

Notes	Monday	Tuesday	Wednesday
	28	29	30
	5	6	7
	12	13	14
	19	20	21
	26	27	28

Thursday	Friday	Saturday	Sunday
1 ☽	2	3	4
8	9	10 ●	11
15	16	17 ☾	18
22	23	24 ○	25
29	30	31 ☽	1

July
Buck moon

July goals

Use this space to write your goals for the month ahead, and any steps you can take that will get you to where you want to be.

Thursday | 1 July 2021

6:00	
7:00	
8:00	
9:00	
10:00	
11:00	
12:00	
13:00	
14:00	
15:00	
16:00	
17:00	
18:00	
19:00	
20:00	
21:00	
22:00	
23:00	
Notes	

Today's quick wins

Health and nutrition

Today, I am grateful for...

Today's self care

Chart your cycle

Positive affirmation

Friday | 2 July 2021

6:00	**Today's quick wins**
7:00	
8:00	
9:00	
10:00	
11:00	**Health and nutrition**
12:00	
13:00	
14:00	**Today, I am grateful for...**
15:00	
16:00	
17:00	**Today's self care**
18:00	
19:00	
20:00	**Chart your cycle**
21:00	
22:00	
23:00	**Positive affirmation**

Notes

Saturday | 3 July 2021

6:00	**Today's quick wins**
7:00	
8:00	
9:00	
10:00	
11:00	**Health and nutrition**
12:00	
13:00	
14:00	**Today, I am grateful for...**
15:00	
16:00	
17:00	**Today's self care**
18:00	
19:00	
20:00	**Chart your cycle**
21:00	
22:00	
23:00	**Positive affirmation**
Notes	

Sunday | 4 July 2021

6:00	**Today's quick wins**
7:00	
8:00	
9:00	
10:00	
11:00	**Health and nutrition**
12:00	
13:00	
14:00	**Today, I am grateful for...**
15:00	
16:00	
17:00	**Today's self care**
18:00	
19:00	
20:00	**Chart your cycle**
21:00	
22:00	
23:00	**Positive affirmation**
Notes	

Monday | 5 July 2021

6:00	**Today's quick wins**
7:00	
8:00	
9:00	
10:00	
11:00	**Health and nutrition**
12:00	
13:00	
14:00	**Today, I am grateful for...**
15:00	
16:00	
17:00	**Today's self care**
18:00	
19:00	
20:00	**Chart your cycle**
21:00	
22:00	
23:00	**Positive affirmation**
Notes	

Tuesday | 6 July 2021

6:00	**Today's quick wins**
7:00	
8:00	
9:00	
10:00	
11:00	**Health and nutrition**
12:00	
13:00	
14:00	**Today, I am grateful for...**
15:00	
16:00	
17:00	**Today's self care**
18:00	
19:00	
20:00	**Chart your cycle**
21:00	
22:00	
23:00	**Positive affirmation**
Notes	

Wednesday | 7 July 2021

6:00	
7:00	
8:00	
9:00	
10:00	
11:00	
12:00	
13:00	
14:00	
15:00	
16:00	
17:00	
18:00	
19:00	
20:00	
21:00	
22:00	
23:00	

Today's quick wins

Health and nutrition

Today, I am grateful for...

Today's self care

Chart your cycle

Positive affirmation

Notes

Thursday | 8 July 2021

6:00	
7:00	
8:00	
9:00	
10:00	
11:00	
12:00	
13:00	
14:00	
15:00	
16:00	
17:00	
18:00	
19:00	
20:00	
21:00	
22:00	
23:00	

Today's quick wins

Health and nutrition

Today, I am grateful for...

Today's self care

Chart your cycle

Positive affirmation

Notes

Friday | 9 July 2021

6:00	**Today's quick wins**
7:00	
8:00	
9:00	
10:00	
11:00	**Health and nutrition**
12:00	
13:00	
14:00	**Today, I am grateful for...**
15:00	
16:00	
17:00	**Today's self care**
18:00	
19:00	
20:00	**Chart your cycle**
21:00	
22:00	
23:00	**Positive affirmation**
Notes	

Saturday | 10 July 2021

6:00	**Today's quick wins**
7:00	
8:00	
9:00	
10:00	
11:00	**Health and nutrition**
12:00	
13:00	
14:00	**Today, I am grateful for...**
15:00	
16:00	
17:00	**Today's self care**
18:00	
19:00	
20:00	**Chart your cycle**
21:00	
22:00	
23:00	**Positive affirmation**
Notes	

Sunday | 11 July 2021

6:00	**Today's quick wins**
7:00	
8:00	
9:00	
10:00	
11:00	**Health and nutrition**
12:00	
13:00	
14:00	**Today, I am grateful for...**
15:00	
16:00	
17:00	**Today's self care**
18:00	
19:00	
20:00	**Chart your cycle**
21:00	
22:00	
23:00	**Positive affirmation**
Notes	

Monday | 12 July 2021

6:00	**Today's quick wins**
7:00	
8:00	
9:00	
10:00	
11:00	**Health and nutrition**
12:00	
13:00	
14:00	**Today, I am grateful for...**
15:00	
16:00	
17:00	**Today's self care**
18:00	
19:00	
20:00	**Chart your cycle**
21:00	
22:00	
23:00	**Positive affirmation**
Notes	

Tuesday | 13 July 2021

6:00	**Today's quick wins**
7:00	
8:00	
9:00	
10:00	
11:00	**Health and nutrition**
12:00	
13:00	
14:00	**Today, I am grateful for...**
15:00	
16:00	
17:00	**Today's self care**
18:00	
19:00	
20:00	**Chart your cycle**
21:00	
22:00	
23:00	**Positive affirmation**
Notes	

Wednesday | 14 July 2021

6:00	
7:00	
8:00	
9:00	
10:00	
11:00	
12:00	
13:00	
14:00	
15:00	
16:00	
17:00	
18:00	
19:00	
20:00	
21:00	
22:00	
23:00	

Notes

Today's quick wins

Health and nutrition

Today, I am grateful for...

Today's self care

Chart your cycle

Positive affirmation

Thursday | 15 July 2021

6:00	**Today's quick wins**
7:00	
8:00	
9:00	
10:00	
11:00	**Health and nutrition**
12:00	
13:00	
14:00	**Today, I am grateful for...**
15:00	
16:00	
17:00	**Today's self care**
18:00	
19:00	
20:00	**Chart your cycle**
21:00	
22:00	
23:00	**Positive affirmation**
Notes	

Friday | 16 July 2021

6:00	**Today's quick wins**
7:00	
8:00	
9:00	
10:00	
11:00	**Health and nutrition**
12:00	
13:00	
14:00	**Today, I am grateful for...**
15:00	
16:00	
17:00	**Today's self care**
18:00	
19:00	
20:00	**Chart your cycle**
21:00	
22:00	
23:00	**Positive affirmation**
Notes	

Saturday | 17 July 2021

6:00	**Today's quick wins**
7:00	
8:00	
9:00	
10:00	
11:00	**Health and nutrition**
12:00	
13:00	
14:00	**Today, I am grateful for...**
15:00	
16:00	
17:00	**Today's self care**
18:00	
19:00	
20:00	**Chart your cycle**
21:00	
22:00	
23:00	**Positive affirmation**
Notes	

Sunday | 18 July 2021

6:00	**Today's quick wins**
7:00	
8:00	
9:00	
10:00	
11:00	**Health and nutrition**
12:00	
13:00	
14:00	**Today, I am grateful for...**
15:00	
16:00	
17:00	**Today's self care**
18:00	
19:00	
20:00	**Chart your cycle**
21:00	
22:00	
23:00	**Positive affirmation**
Notes	

Monday | 19 July 2021

6:00	**Today's quick wins**
7:00	
8:00	
9:00	
10:00	
11:00	**Health and nutrition**
12:00	
13:00	
14:00	**Today, I am grateful for...**
15:00	
16:00	
17:00	**Today's self care**
18:00	
19:00	
20:00	**Chart your cycle**
21:00	
22:00	
23:00	**Positive affirmation**
Notes	

Tuesday | 20 July 2021

6:00	**Today's quick wins**
7:00	
8:00	
9:00	
10:00	
11:00	**Health and nutrition**
12:00	
13:00	
14:00	**Today, I am grateful for...**
15:00	
16:00	
17:00	**Today's self care**
18:00	
19:00	
20:00	**Chart your cycle**
21:00	
22:00	
23:00	**Positive affirmation**
Notes	

Wednesday | 21 July 2021

6:00	**Today's quick wins**
7:00	
8:00	
9:00	
10:00	
11:00	**Health and nutrition**
12:00	
13:00	
14:00	**Today, I am grateful for...**
15:00	
16:00	
17:00	**Today's self care**
18:00	
19:00	
20:00	**Chart your cycle**
21:00	
22:00	
23:00	**Positive affirmation**
Notes	

Thursday | 22 July 2021

6:00	**Today's quick wins**
7:00	
8:00	
9:00	
10:00	
11:00	**Health and nutrition**
12:00	
13:00	
14:00	**Today, I am grateful for...**
15:00	
16:00	
17:00	**Today's self care**
18:00	
19:00	
20:00	**Chart your cycle**
21:00	
22:00	
23:00	**Positive affirmation**
Notes	

Friday | 23 July 2021

6:00	**Today's quick wins**
7:00	
8:00	
9:00	
10:00	
11:00	**Health and nutrition**
12:00	
13:00	
14:00	**Today, I am grateful for...**
15:00	
16:00	
17:00	**Today's self care**
18:00	
19:00	
20:00	**Chart your cycle**
21:00	
22:00	
23:00	**Positive affirmation**
Notes	

Saturday | 24 July 2021

6:00	**Today's quick wins**
7:00	
8:00	
9:00	
10:00	
11:00	**Health and nutrition**
12:00	
13:00	
14:00	**Today, I am grateful for...**
15:00	
16:00	
17:00	**Today's self care**
18:00	
19:00	
20:00	**Chart your cycle**
21:00	
22:00	
23:00	**Positive affirmation**
Notes	

Sunday | 25 July 2021

6:00	**Today's quick wins**
7:00	
8:00	
9:00	
10:00	
11:00	**Health and nutrition**
12:00	
13:00	
14:00	**Today, I am grateful for...**
15:00	
16:00	
17:00	**Today's self care**
18:00	
19:00	
20:00	**Chart your cycle**
21:00	
22:00	
23:00	**Positive affirmation**
Notes	

Monday | 26 July 2021

6:00	**Today's quick wins**
7:00	
8:00	
9:00	
10:00	
11:00	**Health and nutrition**
12:00	
13:00	
14:00	**Today, I am grateful for...**
15:00	
16:00	
17:00	**Today's self care**
18:00	
19:00	
20:00	**Chart your cycle**
21:00	
22:00	
23:00	**Positive affirmation**
Notes	

Tuesday | 27 July 2021

6:00	
7:00	
8:00	
9:00	
10:00	
11:00	
12:00	
13:00	
14:00	
15:00	
16:00	
17:00	
18:00	
19:00	
20:00	
21:00	
22:00	
23:00	
Notes	

Today's quick wins

Health and nutrition

Today, I am grateful for...

Today's self care

Chart your cycle

Positive affirmation

Wednesday | 28 July 2021

6:00	**Today's quick wins**
7:00	
8:00	
9:00	
10:00	
11:00	**Health and nutrition**
12:00	
13:00	
14:00	**Today, I am grateful for...**
15:00	
16:00	
17:00	**Today's self care**
18:00	
19:00	
20:00	**Chart your cycle**
21:00	
22:00	
23:00	**Positive affirmation**
Notes	

Thursday | 29 July 2021

6:00	**Today's quick wins**
7:00	
8:00	
9:00	
10:00	
11:00	**Health and nutrition**
12:00	
13:00	
14:00	**Today, I am grateful for...**
15:00	
16:00	
17:00	**Today's self care**
18:00	
19:00	
20:00	**Chart your cycle**
21:00	
22:00	
23:00	**Positive affirmation**
Notes	

Friday | 30 July 2021

6:00	
7:00	
8:00	
9:00	
10:00	
11:00	
12:00	
13:00	
14:00	
15:00	
16:00	
17:00	
18:00	
19:00	
20:00	
21:00	
22:00	
23:00	

Today's quick wins

Health and nutrition

Today, I am grateful for...

Today's self care

Chart your cycle

Positive affirmation

Notes

Saturday | 31 July 2021

6:00	**Today's quick wins**
7:00	
8:00	
9:00	
10:00	
11:00	**Health and nutrition**
12:00	
13:00	
14:00	**Today, I am grateful for...**
15:00	
16:00	
17:00	**Today's self care**
18:00	
19:00	
20:00	**Chart your cycle**
21:00	
22:00	
23:00	**Positive affirmation**
Notes	

July achievements

Be proud of yourself and all that you have achieved this month. Write down your wins, big and small. If you have not achieved everything that you set out to do, that's okay! We learn and grow through our mistakes and experiences. You can use this space to make notes about anything that you have learned.

August 2021

Sunday	Monday	Tuesday	Wednesday
1	2	3	4
8 ●	9	10	11
15 ◗	16	17	18
22 ○	23	24	25
29	30 ◖	31	

Thursday	Friday	Saturday	Notes
5	6	7	
12	13	14	
19	20	21	
26	27	28	
2	3	4	

August

Sturgeon
moon

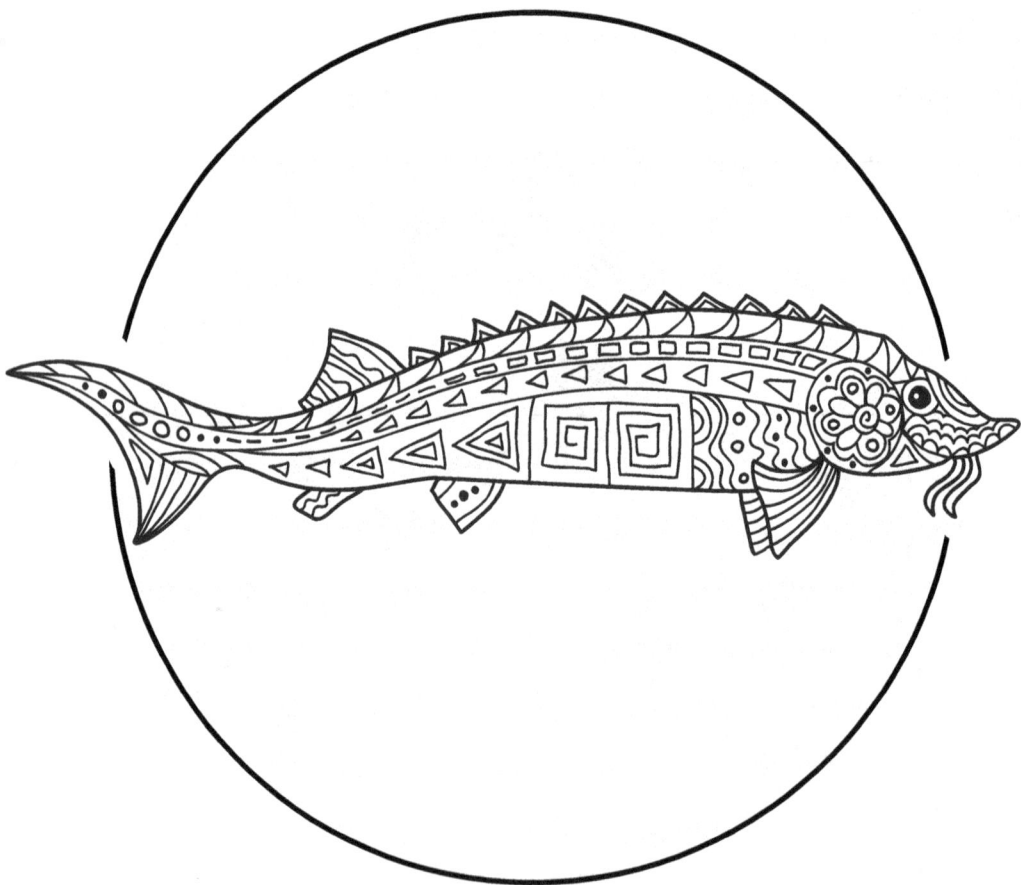

August goals

Use this space to write your goals for the month ahead, and any steps you can take that will get you to where you want to be.

Sunday | 1 August 2021

6:00	**Today's quick wins**
7:00	
8:00	
9:00	
10:00	
11:00	**Health and nutrition**
12:00	
13:00	
14:00	**Today, I am grateful for...**
15:00	
16:00	
17:00	**Today's self care**
18:00	
19:00	
20:00	**Chart your cycle**
21:00	
22:00	
23:00	**Positive affirmation**

Notes

Monday | 2 August 2021

★ ★

6:00	
7:00	
8:00	
9:00	
10:00	
11:00	
12:00	
13:00	
14:00	
15:00	
16:00	
17:00	
18:00	
19:00	
20:00	
21:00	
22:00	
23:00	

Today's quick wins

Health and nutrition

Today, I am grateful for...

Today's self care

Chart your cycle

Positive affirmation

Notes

Tuesday | 3 August 2021

6:00	
7:00	
8:00	
9:00	
10:00	
11:00	
12:00	
13:00	
14:00	
15:00	
16:00	
17:00	
18:00	
19:00	
20:00	
21:00	
22:00	
23:00	

Notes

Today's quick wins

Health and nutrition

Today, I am grateful for...

Today's self care

Chart your cycle

Positive affirmation

Wednesday | 4 August 2021

6:00	**Today's quick wins**
7:00	
8:00	
9:00	
10:00	
11:00	**Health and nutrition**
12:00	
13:00	
14:00	**Today, I am grateful for...**
15:00	
16:00	
17:00	**Today's self care**
18:00	
19:00	
20:00	**Chart your cycle**
21:00	
22:00	
23:00	**Positive affirmation**
Notes	

Thursday | 5 August 2021

6:00	**Today's quick wins**
7:00	
8:00	
9:00	
10:00	
11:00	**Health and nutrition**
12:00	
13:00	
14:00	**Today, I am grateful for...**
15:00	
16:00	
17:00	**Today's self care**
18:00	
19:00	
20:00	**Chart your cycle**
21:00	
22:00	
23:00	**Positive affirmation**
Notes	

Friday | 6 August 2021

6:00	**Today's quick wins**
7:00	
8:00	
9:00	
10:00	
11:00	**Health and nutrition**
12:00	
13:00	
14:00	**Today, I am grateful for...**
15:00	
16:00	
17:00	**Today's self care**
18:00	
19:00	
20:00	**Chart your cycle**
21:00	
22:00	
23:00	**Positive affirmation**
Notes	

Saturday | 7 August 2021

6:00	**Today's quick wins**
7:00	
8:00	
9:00	
10:00	
11:00	**Health and nutrition**
12:00	
13:00	
14:00	**Today, I am grateful for...**
15:00	
16:00	
17:00	**Today's self care**
18:00	
19:00	
20:00	**Chart your cycle**
21:00	
22:00	
23:00	**Positive affirmation**
Notes	

Sunday | 8 August 2021

6:00	
7:00	
8:00	
9:00	
10:00	
11:00	
12:00	
13:00	
14:00	
15:00	
16:00	
17:00	
18:00	
19:00	
20:00	
21:00	
22:00	
23:00	

Today's quick wins

Health and nutrition

Today, I am grateful for...

Today's self care

Chart your cycle

Positive affirmation

Notes

Monday | 9 August 2021

6:00	**Today's quick wins**
7:00	
8:00	
9:00	
10:00	
11:00	**Health and nutrition**
12:00	
13:00	
14:00	**Today, I am grateful for...**
15:00	
16:00	
17:00	**Today's self care**
18:00	
19:00	
20:00	**Chart your cycle**
21:00	
22:00	
23:00	**Positive affirmation**
Notes	

Tuesday | 10 August 2021

6:00	**Today's quick wins**
7:00	
8:00	
9:00	
10:00	
11:00	**Health and nutrition**
12:00	
13:00	
14:00	**Today, I am grateful for...**
15:00	
16:00	
17:00	**Today's self care**
18:00	
19:00	
20:00	**Chart your cycle**
21:00	
22:00	
23:00	**Positive affirmation**
Notes	

Wednesday | 11 August 2021

6:00	
7:00	
8:00	
9:00	
10:00	
11:00	
12:00	
13:00	
14:00	
15:00	
16:00	
17:00	
18:00	
19:00	
20:00	
21:00	
22:00	
23:00	

Notes

Today's quick wins

Health and nutrition

Today, I am grateful for...

Today's self care

Chart your cycle

Positive affirmation

Thursday | 12 August 2021

6:00	**Today's quick wins**
7:00	
8:00	
9:00	
10:00	
11:00	**Health and nutrition**
12:00	
13:00	
14:00	**Today, I am grateful for...**
15:00	
16:00	
17:00	**Today's self care**
18:00	
19:00	
20:00	**Chart your cycle**
21:00	
22:00	
23:00	**Positive affirmation**
Notes	

Friday | 13 August 2021

6:00	**Today's quick wins**
7:00	
8:00	
9:00	
10:00	
11:00	**Health and nutrition**
12:00	
13:00	
14:00	**Today, I am grateful for...**
15:00	
16:00	
17:00	**Today's self care**
18:00	
19:00	
20:00	**Chart your cycle**
21:00	
22:00	
23:00	**Positive affirmation**
Notes	

Saturday | 14 August 2021

6:00	**Today's quick wins**
7:00	
8:00	
9:00	
10:00	
11:00	**Health and nutrition**
12:00	
13:00	
14:00	**Today, I am grateful for...**
15:00	
16:00	
17:00	**Today's self care**
18:00	
19:00	
20:00	**Chart your cycle**
21:00	
22:00	
23:00	**Positive affirmation**
Notes	

Sunday | 15 August 2021

6:00	**Today's quick wins**
7:00	
8:00	
9:00	
10:00	
11:00	**Health and nutrition**
12:00	
13:00	
14:00	**Today, I am grateful for...**
15:00	
16:00	
17:00	**Today's self care**
18:00	
19:00	
20:00	**Chart your cycle**
21:00	
22:00	
23:00	**Positive affirmation**
Notes	

Monday | 16 August 2021

6:00	**Today's quick wins**
7:00	
8:00	
9:00	
10:00	
11:00	**Health and nutrition**
12:00	
13:00	
14:00	**Today, I am grateful for...**
15:00	
16:00	
17:00	**Today's self care**
18:00	
19:00	
20:00	**Chart your cycle**
21:00	
22:00	
23:00	**Positive affirmation**
Notes	

Tuesday | 17 August 2021

6:00	**Today's quick wins**
7:00	
8:00	
9:00	
10:00	
11:00	**Health and nutrition**
12:00	
13:00	
14:00	**Today, I am grateful for...**
15:00	
16:00	
17:00	**Today's self care**
18:00	
19:00	
20:00	**Chart your cycle**
21:00	
22:00	
23:00	**Positive affirmation**
Notes	

Wednesday | 18 August 2021

6:00	**Today's quick wins**
7:00	
8:00	
9:00	
10:00	
11:00	**Health and nutrition**
12:00	
13:00	
14:00	**Today, I am grateful for...**
15:00	
16:00	
17:00	**Today's self care**
18:00	
19:00	
20:00	**Chart your cycle**
21:00	
22:00	
23:00	**Positive affirmation**
Notes	

Thursday | 19 August 2021

6:00	**Today's quick wins**
7:00	
8:00	
9:00	
10:00	
11:00	**Health and nutrition**
12:00	
13:00	
14:00	**Today, I am grateful for...**
15:00	
16:00	
17:00	**Today's self care**
18:00	
19:00	
20:00	**Chart your cycle**
21:00	
22:00	
23:00	**Positive affirmation**
Notes	

Friday | 20 August 2021

6:00	**Today's quick wins**
7:00	
8:00	
9:00	
10:00	
11:00	**Health and nutrition**
12:00	
13:00	
14:00	**Today, I am grateful for...**
15:00	
16:00	
17:00	**Today's self care**
18:00	
19:00	
20:00	**Chart your cycle**
21:00	
22:00	
23:00	**Positive affirmation**
Notes	

Saturday | 21 August 2021

6:00	**Today's quick wins**
7:00	
8:00	
9:00	
10:00	
11:00	**Health and nutrition**
12:00	
13:00	
14:00	**Today, I am grateful for...**
15:00	
16:00	
17:00	**Today's self care**
18:00	
19:00	
20:00	**Chart your cycle**
21:00	
22:00	
23:00	**Positive affirmation**
Notes	

Sunday | 22 August 2021

6:00	**Today's quick wins**
7:00	
8:00	
9:00	
10:00	
11:00	**Health and nutrition**
12:00	
13:00	
14:00	**Today, I am grateful for...**
15:00	
16:00	
17:00	**Today's self care**
18:00	
19:00	
20:00	**Chart your cycle**
21:00	
22:00	
23:00	**Positive affirmation**

Notes

Monday | 23 August 2021

6:00	**Today's quick wins**
7:00	
8:00	
9:00	
10:00	
11:00	**Health and nutrition**
12:00	
13:00	
14:00	**Today, I am grateful for...**
15:00	
16:00	
17:00	**Today's self care**
18:00	
19:00	
20:00	**Chart your cycle**
21:00	
22:00	
23:00	**Positive affirmation**
Notes	

Tuesday | 24 August 2021

6:00	**Today's quick wins**
7:00	
8:00	
9:00	
10:00	
11:00	**Health and nutrition**
12:00	
13:00	
14:00	**Today, I am grateful for...**
15:00	
16:00	
17:00	**Today's self care**
18:00	
19:00	
20:00	**Chart your cycle**
21:00	
22:00	
23:00	**Positive affirmation**
Notes	

Wednesday | 25 August 2021

6:00	**Today's quick wins**
7:00	
8:00	
9:00	
10:00	
11:00	**Health and nutrition**
12:00	
13:00	
14:00	**Today, I am grateful for...**
15:00	
16:00	
17:00	**Today's self care**
18:00	
19:00	
20:00	**Chart your cycle**
21:00	
22:00	
23:00	**Positive affirmation**
Notes	

Thursday | 26 August 2021

6:00	**Today's quick wins**
7:00	
8:00	
9:00	
10:00	
11:00	**Health and nutrition**
12:00	
13:00	
14:00	**Today, I am grateful for...**
15:00	
16:00	
17:00	**Today's self care**
18:00	
19:00	
20:00	**Chart your cycle**
21:00	
22:00	
23:00	**Positive affirmation**
Notes	

Friday | 27 August 2021

6:00	**Today's quick wins**
7:00	
8:00	
9:00	
10:00	
11:00	**Health and nutrition**
12:00	
13:00	
14:00	**Today, I am grateful for...**
15:00	
16:00	
17:00	**Today's self care**
18:00	
19:00	
20:00	**Chart your cycle**
21:00	
22:00	
23:00	**Positive affirmation**
Notes	

Saturday | 28 August 2021

6:00	**Today's quick wins**
7:00	
8:00	
9:00	
10:00	
11:00	**Health and nutrition**
12:00	
13:00	
14:00	**Today, I am grateful for...**
15:00	
16:00	
17:00	**Today's self care**
18:00	
19:00	
20:00	**Chart your cycle**
21:00	
22:00	
23:00	**Positive affirmation**
Notes	

Sunday | 29 August 2021

6:00	**Today's quick wins**
7:00	
8:00	
9:00	
10:00	
11:00	**Health and nutrition**
12:00	
13:00	
14:00	**Today, I am grateful for...**
15:00	
16:00	
17:00	**Today's self care**
18:00	
19:00	
20:00	**Chart your cycle**
21:00	
22:00	
23:00	**Positive affirmation**
Notes	

Monday | 30 August 2021

6:00	**Today's quick wins**
7:00	
8:00	
9:00	
10:00	
11:00	**Health and nutrition**
12:00	
13:00	
14:00	**Today, I am grateful for...**
15:00	
16:00	
17:00	**Today's self care**
18:00	
19:00	
20:00	**Chart your cycle**
21:00	
22:00	
23:00	**Positive affirmation**
Notes	

Tuesday | 31 August 2021

6:00	**Today's quick wins**
7:00	
8:00	
9:00	
10:00	
11:00	**Health and nutrition**
12:00	
13:00	
14:00	**Today, I am grateful for...**
15:00	
16:00	
17:00	**Today's self care**
18:00	
19:00	
20:00	**Chart your cycle**
21:00	
22:00	
23:00	**Positive affirmation**
Notes	

August achievements

Be proud of yourself and all that you have achieved this month. Write down your wins, big and small. If you have not achieved everything that you set out to do, that's okay! We learn and grow through our mistakes and experiences. You can use this space to make notes about anything that you have learned.

September 2021

Notes	Monday	Tuesday	Wednesday
	30	31	1
	6	7 ●	8
	13 ◗	14	15
	20 ○	21	22 *Autumn equinox*
	27	28	29 ◗

Thursday	Friday	Saturday	Sunday
2	3	4	5
9	10	11	12
16	17	18	19
23	24	25	26
30	1	2	3

September
Full Corn
moon

September goals

Use this space to write your goals for the month ahead, and any steps you can take that will get you to where you want to be.

Wednesday | 1 September 2021

6:00	
7:00	
8:00	
9:00	
10:00	
11:00	
12:00	
13:00	
14:00	
15:00	
16:00	
17:00	
18:00	
19:00	
20:00	
21:00	
22:00	
23:00	

Today's quick wins

Health and nutrition

Today, I am grateful for...

Today's self care

Chart your cycle

Positive affirmation

Notes

Thursday | 2 September 2021

6:00	
7:00	
8:00	
9:00	
10:00	
11:00	
12:00	
13:00	
14:00	
15:00	
16:00	
17:00	
18:00	
19:00	
20:00	
21:00	
22:00	
23:00	

Today's quick wins

Health and nutrition

Today, I am grateful for...

Today's self care

Chart your cycle

Positive affirmation

Notes

Friday | 3 September 2021

6:00	**Today's quick wins**
7:00	
8:00	
9:00	
10:00	
11:00	**Health and nutrition**
12:00	
13:00	
14:00	**Today, I am grateful for...**
15:00	
16:00	
17:00	**Today's self care**
18:00	
19:00	
20:00	**Chart your cycle**
21:00	
22:00	
23:00	**Positive affirmation**
Notes	

Saturday | 4 September 2021

6:00	**Today's quick wins**
7:00	
8:00	
9:00	
10:00	
11:00	**Health and nutrition**
12:00	
13:00	
14:00	**Today, I am grateful for...**
15:00	
16:00	
17:00	**Today's self care**
18:00	
19:00	
20:00	**Chart your cycle**
21:00	
22:00	
23:00	**Positive affirmation**

Notes

Sunday | 5 September 2021

6:00	**Today's quick wins**
7:00	
8:00	
9:00	
10:00	
11:00	**Health and nutrition**
12:00	
13:00	
14:00	**Today, I am grateful for...**
15:00	
16:00	
17:00	**Today's self care**
18:00	
19:00	
20:00	**Chart your cycle**
21:00	
22:00	
23:00	**Positive affirmation**
Notes	

Monday | 6 September 2021

6:00	**Today's quick wins**
7:00	
8:00	
9:00	
10:00	
11:00	**Health and nutrition**
12:00	
13:00	
14:00	**Today, I am grateful for...**
15:00	
16:00	
17:00	**Today's self care**
18:00	
19:00	
20:00	**Chart your cycle**
21:00	
22:00	
23:00	**Positive affirmation**
Notes	

Tuesday | 7 September 2021

6:00	**Today's quick wins**
7:00	
8:00	
9:00	
10:00	
11:00	**Health and nutrition**
12:00	
13:00	
14:00	**Today, I am grateful for...**
15:00	
16:00	
17:00	**Today's self care**
18:00	
19:00	
20:00	**Chart your cycle**
21:00	
22:00	
23:00	**Positive affirmation**
Notes	

Wednesday | 8 September 2021

6:00	**Today's quick wins**
7:00	
8:00	
9:00	
10:00	
11:00	**Health and nutrition**
12:00	
13:00	
14:00	**Today, I am grateful for...**
15:00	
16:00	
17:00	**Today's self care**
18:00	
19:00	
20:00	**Chart your cycle**
21:00	
22:00	
23:00	**Positive affirmation**
Notes	

Thursday | 9 September 2021

6:00	**Today's quick wins**
7:00	
8:00	
9:00	
10:00	
11:00	**Health and nutrition**
12:00	
13:00	
14:00	**Today, I am grateful for...**
15:00	
16:00	
17:00	**Today's self care**
18:00	
19:00	
20:00	**Chart your cycle**
21:00	
22:00	
23:00	**Positive affirmation**
Notes	

Friday | 10 September 2021

6:00	**Today's quick wins**
7:00	
8:00	
9:00	
10:00	
11:00	**Health and nutrition**
12:00	
13:00	
14:00	**Today, I am grateful for...**
15:00	
16:00	
17:00	**Today's self care**
18:00	
19:00	
20:00	**Chart your cycle**
21:00	
22:00	
23:00	**Positive affirmation**
Notes	

Saturday | 11 September 2021

6:00	**Today's quick wins**
7:00	
8:00	
9:00	
10:00	
11:00	**Health and nutrition**
12:00	
13:00	
14:00	**Today, I am grateful for...**
15:00	
16:00	
17:00	**Today's self care**
18:00	
19:00	
20:00	**Chart your cycle**
21:00	
22:00	
23:00	**Positive affirmation**
Notes	

Sunday | 12 September 2021

6:00	**Today's quick wins**
7:00	
8:00	
9:00	
10:00	
11:00	**Health and nutrition**
12:00	
13:00	
14:00	**Today, I am grateful for...**
15:00	
16:00	
17:00	**Today's self care**
18:00	
19:00	
20:00	**Chart your cycle**
21:00	
22:00	
23:00	**Positive affirmation**
Notes	

Monday | 13 September 2021

6:00	**Today's quick wins**
7:00	
8:00	
9:00	
10:00	
11:00	**Health and nutrition**
12:00	
13:00	
14:00	**Today, I am grateful for...**
15:00	
16:00	
17:00	**Today's self care**
18:00	
19:00	
20:00	**Chart your cycle**
21:00	
22:00	
23:00	**Positive affirmation**
Notes	

Tuesday | 14 September 2021

6:00	
7:00	
8:00	
9:00	
10:00	
11:00	
12:00	
13:00	
14:00	
15:00	
16:00	
17:00	
18:00	
19:00	
20:00	
21:00	
22:00	
23:00	

Today's quick wins

Health and nutrition

Today, I am grateful for...

Today's self care

Chart your cycle

Positive affirmation

Notes

Wednesday | 15 September 2021

6:00	
7:00	
8:00	
9:00	
10:00	
11:00	
12:00	
13:00	
14:00	
15:00	
16:00	
17:00	
18:00	
19:00	
20:00	
21:00	
22:00	
23:00	

Notes

Today's quick wins

Health and nutrition

Today, I am grateful for...

Today's self care

Chart your cycle

Positive affirmation

Thursday | 16 September 2021

6:00	**Today's quick wins**
7:00	
8:00	
9:00	
10:00	
11:00	**Health and nutrition**
12:00	
13:00	
14:00	**Today, I am grateful for...**
15:00	
16:00	
17:00	**Today's self care**
18:00	
19:00	
20:00	**Chart your cycle**
21:00	
22:00	
23:00	**Positive affirmation**
Notes	

Friday | 17 September 2021

6:00	**Today's quick wins**
7:00	
8:00	
9:00	
10:00	
11:00	**Health and nutrition**
12:00	
13:00	
14:00	**Today, I am grateful for...**
15:00	
16:00	
17:00	**Today's self care**
18:00	
19:00	
20:00	**Chart your cycle**
21:00	
22:00	
23:00	**Positive affirmation**
Notes	

Saturday | 18 September 2021

6:00	
7:00	
8:00	
9:00	
10:00	
11:00	
12:00	
13:00	
14:00	
15:00	
16:00	
17:00	
18:00	
19:00	
20:00	
21:00	
22:00	
23:00	

Today's quick wins

Health and nutrition

Today, I am grateful for...

Today's self care

Chart your cycle

Positive affirmation

Notes

Sunday | 19 September 2021

6:00	**Today's quick wins**	
7:00		
8:00		
9:00		
10:00		
11:00	**Health and nutrition**	
12:00		
13:00		
14:00	**Today, I am grateful for...**	
15:00		
16:00		
17:00	**Today's self care**	
18:00		
19:00		
20:00	**Chart your cycle**	
21:00		
22:00		
23:00	**Positive affirmation**	
Notes		

Monday | 20 September 2021

6:00	**Today's quick wins**
7:00	
8:00	
9:00	
10:00	
11:00	**Health and nutrition**
12:00	
13:00	
14:00	**Today, I am grateful for...**
15:00	
16:00	
17:00	**Today's self care**
18:00	
19:00	
20:00	**Chart your cycle**
21:00	
22:00	
23:00	**Positive affirmation**
Notes	

Tuesday | 21 September 2021

6:00	**Today's quick wins**
7:00	
8:00	
9:00	
10:00	
11:00	**Health and nutrition**
12:00	
13:00	
14:00	**Today, I am grateful for...**
15:00	
16:00	
17:00	**Today's self care**
18:00	
19:00	
20:00	**Chart your cycle**
21:00	
22:00	
23:00	**Positive affirmation**
Notes	

Wednesday | 22 September 2021

6:00	**Today's quick wins**
7:00	
8:00	
9:00	
10:00	
11:00	**Health and nutrition**
12:00	
13:00	
14:00	**Today, I am grateful for...**
15:00	
16:00	
17:00	**Today's self care**
18:00	
19:00	
20:00	**Chart your cycle**
21:00	
22:00	
23:00	**Positive affirmation**
Notes	

Thursday | 23 September 2021

6:00	**Today's quick wins**
7:00	
8:00	
9:00	
10:00	
11:00	**Health and nutrition**
12:00	
13:00	
14:00	**Today, I am grateful for...**
15:00	
16:00	
17:00	**Today's self care**
18:00	
19:00	
20:00	**Chart your cycle**
21:00	
22:00	
23:00	**Positive affirmation**
Notes	

Friday | 24 September 2021

6:00	**Today's quick wins**
7:00	
8:00	
9:00	
10:00	
11:00	**Health and nutrition**
12:00	
13:00	
14:00	**Today, I am grateful for...**
15:00	
16:00	
17:00	**Today's self care**
18:00	
19:00	
20:00	**Chart your cycle**
21:00	
22:00	
23:00	**Positive affirmation**
Notes	

Saturday | 25 September 2021

6:00	**Today's quick wins**
7:00	
8:00	
9:00	
10:00	
11:00	**Health and nutrition**
12:00	
13:00	
14:00	**Today, I am grateful for...**
15:00	
16:00	
17:00	**Today's self care**
18:00	
19:00	
20:00	**Chart your cycle**
21:00	
22:00	
23:00	**Positive affirmation**
Notes	

Sunday | 26 September 2021

6:00	
7:00	
8:00	
9:00	
10:00	
11:00	
12:00	
13:00	
14:00	
15:00	
16:00	
17:00	
18:00	
19:00	
20:00	
21:00	
22:00	
23:00	

Today's quick wins

Health and nutrition

Today, I am grateful for...

Today's self care

Chart your cycle

Positive affirmation

Notes

Monday | 27 September 2021

6:00	**Today's quick wins**
7:00	
8:00	
9:00	
10:00	
11:00	**Health and nutrition**
12:00	
13:00	
14:00	**Today, I am grateful for...**
15:00	
16:00	
17:00	**Today's self care**
18:00	
19:00	
20:00	**Chart your cycle**
21:00	
22:00	
23:00	**Positive affirmation**
Notes	

Tuesday | 28 September 2021

6:00	**Today's quick wins**
7:00	
8:00	
9:00	
10:00	
11:00	**Health and nutrition**
12:00	
13:00	
14:00	**Today, I am grateful for...**
15:00	
16:00	
17:00	**Today's self care**
18:00	
19:00	
20:00	**Chart your cycle**
21:00	
22:00	
23:00	**Positive affirmation**
Notes	

Wednesday | 29 September 2021

6:00	**Today's quick wins**
7:00	
8:00	
9:00	
10:00	
11:00	**Health and nutrition**
12:00	
13:00	
14:00	**Today, I am grateful for...**
15:00	
16:00	
17:00	**Today's self care**
18:00	
19:00	
20:00	**Chart your cycle**
21:00	
22:00	
23:00	**Positive affirmation**
Notes	

Thursday | 30 September 2021

6:00	**Today's quick wins**
7:00	
8:00	
9:00	
10:00	
11:00	**Health and nutrition**
12:00	
13:00	
14:00	**Today, I am grateful for...**
15:00	
16:00	
17:00	**Today's self care**
18:00	
19:00	
20:00	**Chart your cycle**
21:00	
22:00	
23:00	**Positive affirmation**
Notes	

September achievements

Be proud of yourself and all that you have achieved this month. Write down your wins, big and small. If you have not achieved everything that you set out to do, that's okay! We learn and grow through our mistakes and experiences. You can use this space to make notes about anything that you have learned.

'Find the place inside yourself where nothing is impossible.'

– Deepak Chopra

October 2021

Notes	Monday	Tuesday	Wednesday
	27	28	29
	4	5	6 ●
	11	12	13 ◗
	18	19	20 ○
	25	26	27

Thursday	Friday	Saturday	Sunday
30	1	2	3
7	8	0	10
14	15	16	17
21	22	23	24
28 ☽	29	30	31

October

Hunters
moon

October goals

Use this space to write your goals for the month ahead,
and any steps you can take that will get you to where you
want to be.

Friday | 1 October 2021

6:00		**Today's quick wins**
7:00		
8:00		
9:00		
10:00		
11:00		**Health and nutrition**
12:00		
13:00		
14:00		**Today, I am grateful for...**
15:00		
16:00		
17:00		**Today's self care**
18:00		
19:00		
20:00		**Chart your cycle**
21:00		
22:00		
23:00		**Positive affirmation**
Notes		

Saturday | 2 October 2021

6:00	
7:00	
8:00	
9:00	
10:00	
11:00	
12:00	
13:00	
14:00	
15:00	
16:00	
17:00	
18:00	
19:00	
20:00	
21:00	
22:00	
23:00	

Today's quick wins

Health and nutrition

Today, I am grateful for...

Today's self care

Chart your cycle

Positive affirmation

Notes

Sunday | 3 October 2021

6:00	**Today's quick wins**
7:00	
8:00	
9:00	
10:00	
11:00	**Health and nutrition**
12:00	
13:00	
14:00	**Today, I am grateful for...**
15:00	
16:00	
17:00	**Today's self care**
18:00	
19:00	
20:00	**Chart your cycle**
21:00	
22:00	
23:00	**Positive affirmation**
Notes	

Monday | 4 October 2021

6:00	**Today's quick wins**
7:00	
8:00	
9:00	
10:00	
11:00	**Health and nutrition**
12:00	
13:00	
14:00	**Today, I am grateful for...**
15:00	
16:00	
17:00	**Today's self care**
18:00	
19:00	
20:00	**Chart your cycle**
21:00	
22:00	
23:00	**Positive affirmation**
Notes	

Tuesday | 5 October 2021

6:00	
7:00	
8:00	
9:00	
10:00	
11:00	
12:00	
13:00	
14:00	
15:00	
16:00	
17:00	
18:00	
19:00	
20:00	
21:00	
22:00	
23:00	

Today's quick wins

Health and nutrition

Today, I am grateful for...

Today's self care

Chart your cycle

Positive affirmation

Notes

Wednesday | 6 October 2021

6:00	
7:00	
8:00	
9:00	
10:00	
11:00	
12:00	
13:00	
14:00	
15:00	
16:00	
17:00	
18:00	
19:00	
20:00	
21:00	
22:00	
23:00	

Today's quick wins

Health and nutrition

Today, I am grateful for...

Today's self care

Chart your cycle

Positive affirmation

Notes

Thursday | 7 October 2021

6:00	**Today's quick wins**
7:00	
8:00	
9:00	
10:00	
11:00	**Health and nutrition**
12:00	
13:00	
14:00	**Today, I am grateful for...**
15:00	
16:00	
17:00	**Today's self care**
18:00	
19:00	
20:00	**Chart your cycle**
21:00	
22:00	
23:00	**Positive affirmation**
Notes	

Friday | 8 October 2021

6:00	**Today's quick wins**
7:00	
8:00	
9:00	
10:00	
11:00	**Health and nutrition**
12:00	
13:00	
14:00	**Today, I am grateful for...**
15:00	
16:00	
17:00	**Today's self care**
18:00	
19:00	
20:00	**Chart your cycle**
21:00	
22:00	
23:00	**Positive affirmation**
Notes	

Saturday | 9 October 2021

6:00	**Today's quick wins**
7:00	
8:00	
9:00	
10:00	
11:00	**Health and nutrition**
12:00	
13:00	
14:00	**Today, I am grateful for...**
15:00	
16:00	
17:00	**Today's self care**
18:00	
19:00	
20:00	**Chart your cycle**
21:00	
22:00	
23:00	**Positive affirmation**
Notes	

Sunday | 10 October 2021

6:00	**Today's quick wins**
7:00	
8:00	
9:00	
10:00	
11:00	**Health and nutrition**
12:00	
13:00	
14:00	**Today, I am grateful for...**
15:00	
16:00	
17:00	**Today's self care**
18:00	
19:00	
20:00	**Chart your cycle**
21:00	
22:00	
23:00	**Positive affirmation**
Notes	

Monday | 11 October 2021

6:00	**Today's quick wins**
7:00	
8:00	
9:00	
10:00	
11:00	**Health and nutrition**
12:00	
13:00	
14:00	**Today, I am grateful for...**
15:00	
16:00	
17:00	**Today's self care**
18:00	
19:00	
20:00	**Chart your cycle**
21:00	
22:00	
23:00	**Positive affirmation**
Notes	

Tuesday | 12 October 2021

6:00	**Today's quick wins**
7:00	
8:00	
9:00	
10:00	
11:00	**Health and nutrition**
12:00	
13:00	
14:00	**Today, I am grateful for...**
15:00	
16:00	
17:00	**Today's self care**
18:00	
19:00	
20:00	**Chart your cycle**
21:00	
22:00	
23:00	**Positive affirmation**
Notes	

Wednesday | 13 October 2021

6:00	
7:00	
8:00	
9:00	
10:00	
11:00	
12:00	
13:00	
14:00	
15:00	
16:00	
17:00	
18:00	
19:00	
20:00	
21:00	
22:00	
23:00	

Notes

Today's quick wins

Health and nutrition

Today, I am grateful for...

Today's self care

Chart your cycle

Positive affirmation

Thursday | 14 October 2021

6:00	**Today's quick wins**
7:00	
8:00	
9:00	
10:00	
11:00	**Health and nutrition**
12:00	
13:00	
14:00	**Today, I am grateful for...**
15:00	
16:00	
17:00	**Today's self care**
18:00	
19:00	
20:00	**Chart your cycle**
21:00	
22:00	
23:00	**Positive affirmation**

Notes

Friday | 15 October 2021

6:00	**Today's quick wins**
7:00	
8:00	
9:00	
10:00	
11:00	**Health and nutrition**
12:00	
13:00	
14:00	**Today, I am grateful for...**
15:00	
16:00	
17:00	**Today's self care**
18:00	
19:00	
20:00	**Chart your cycle**
21:00	
22:00	
23:00	**Positive affirmation**
Notes	

Saturday | 16 October 2021

6:00	**Today's quick wins**
7:00	
8:00	
9:00	
10:00	
11:00	**Health and nutrition**
12:00	
13:00	
14:00	**Today, I am grateful for...**
15:00	
16:00	
17:00	**Today's self care**
18:00	
19:00	
20:00	**Chart your cycle**
21:00	
22:00	
23:00	**Positive affirmation**
Notes	

Sunday | 17 October 2021

6:00	**Today's quick wins**
7:00	
8:00	
9:00	
10:00	
11:00	**Health and nutrition**
12:00	
13:00	
14:00	**Today, I am grateful for...**
15:00	
16:00	
17:00	**Today's self care**
18:00	
19:00	
20:00	**Chart your cycle**
21:00	
22:00	
23:00	**Positive affirmation**
Notes	

Monday | 18 October 2021

6:00	
7:00	
8:00	
9:00	
10:00	
11:00	
12:00	
13:00	
14:00	
15:00	
16:00	
17:00	
18:00	
19:00	
20:00	
21:00	
22:00	
23:00	

Today's quick wins

Health and nutrition

Today, I am grateful for...

Today's self care

Chart your cycle

Positive affirmation

Notes

Tuesday | 19 October 2021

6:00	**Today's quick wins**
7:00	
8:00	
9:00	
10:00	
11:00	**Health and nutrition**
12:00	
13:00	
14:00	**Today, I am grateful for...**
15:00	
16:00	
17:00	**Today's self care**
18:00	
19:00	
20:00	**Chart your cycle**
21:00	
22:00	
23:00	**Positive affirmation**
Notes	

Wednesday | 20 October 2021

6:00	**Today's quick wins**
7:00	
8:00	
9:00	
10:00	
11:00	**Health and nutrition**
12:00	
13:00	
14:00	**Today, I am grateful for...**
15:00	
16:00	
17:00	**Today's self care**
18:00	
19:00	
20:00	**Chart your cycle**
21:00	
22:00	
23:00	**Positive affirmation**
Notes	

Thursday | 21 October 2021

6:00	**Today's quick wins**
7:00	
8:00	
9:00	
10:00	
11:00	**Health and nutrition**
12:00	
13:00	
14:00	**Today, I am grateful for...**
15:00	
16:00	
17:00	**Today's self care**
18:00	
19:00	
20:00	**Chart your cycle**
21:00	
22:00	
23:00	**Positive affirmation**
Notes	

Friday | 22 October 2021

6:00	**Today's quick wins**
7:00	
8:00	
9:00	
10:00	
11:00	**Health and nutrition**
12:00	
13:00	
14:00	**Today, I am grateful for...**
15:00	
16:00	
17:00	**Today's self care**
18:00	
19:00	
20:00	**Chart your cycle**
21:00	
22:00	
23:00	**Positive affirmation**
Notes	

Saturday | 23 October 2021

6:00	
7:00	
8:00	
9:00	
10:00	
11:00	
12:00	
13:00	
14:00	
15:00	
16:00	
17:00	
18:00	
19:00	
20:00	
21:00	
22:00	
23:00	

Today's quick wins

Health and nutrition

Today, I am grateful for...

Today's self care

Chart your cycle

Positive affirmation

Notes

Sunday | 24 October 2021

6:00	
7:00	
8:00	
9:00	
10:00	
11:00	
12:00	
13:00	
14:00	
15:00	
16:00	
17:00	
18:00	
19:00	
20:00	
21:00	
22:00	
23:00	

Today's quick wins

Health and nutrition

Today, I am grateful for...

Today's self care

Chart your cycle

Positive affirmation

Notes

Monday | 25 October 2021

6:00	**Today's quick wins**
7:00	
8:00	
9:00	
10:00	
11:00	**Health and nutrition**
12:00	
13:00	
14:00	**Today, I am grateful for...**
15:00	
16:00	
17:00	**Today's self care**
18:00	
19:00	
20:00	**Chart your cycle**
21:00	
22:00	
23:00	**Positive affirmation**
Notes	

Tuesday | 26 October 2021

6:00	**Today's quick wins**
7:00	
8:00	
9:00	
10:00	
11:00	**Health and nutrition**
12:00	
13:00	
14:00	**Today, I am grateful for...**
15:00	
16:00	
17:00	**Today's self care**
18:00	
19:00	
20:00	**Chart your cycle**
21:00	
22:00	
23:00	**Positive affirmation**

Notes

Wednesday | 27 October 2021

6:00	**Today's quick wins**
7:00	
8:00	
9:00	
10:00	
11:00	**Health and nutrition**
12:00	
13:00	
14:00	**Today, I am grateful for...**
15:00	
16:00	
17:00	**Today's self care**
18:00	
19:00	
20:00	**Chart your cycle**
21:00	
22:00	
23:00	**Positive affirmation**
Notes	

Thursday | 28 October 2021

6:00	**Today's quick wins**
7:00	
8:00	
9:00	
10:00	
11:00	**Health and nutrition**
12:00	
13:00	
14:00	**Today, I am grateful for...**
15:00	
16:00	
17:00	**Today's self care**
18:00	
19:00	
20:00	**Chart your cycle**
21:00	
22:00	
23:00	**Positive affirmation**

Notes

Friday | 29 October 2021

6:00	**Today's quick wins**
7:00	
8:00	
9:00	
10:00	
11:00	**Health and nutrition**
12:00	
13:00	
14:00	**Today, I am grateful for...**
15:00	
16:00	
17:00	**Today's self care**
18:00	
19:00	
20:00	**Chart your cycle**
21:00	
22:00	
23:00	**Positive affirmation**
Notes	

Saturday | 30 October 2021

6:00	**Today's quick wins**
7:00	
8:00	
9:00	
10:00	
11:00	**Health and nutrition**
12:00	
13:00	
14:00	**Today, I am grateful for...**
15:00	
16:00	
17:00	**Today's self care**
18:00	
19:00	
20:00	**Chart your cycle**
21:00	
22:00	
23:00	**Positive affirmation**
Notes	

Sunday | 31 October 2021

6:00	**Today's quick wins**
7:00	
8:00	
9:00	
10:00	
11:00	**Health and nutrition**
12:00	
13:00	
14:00	**Today, I am grateful for...**
15:00	
16:00	
17:00	**Today's self care**
18:00	
19:00	
20:00	**Chart your cycle**
21:00	
22:00	
23:00	**Positive affirmation**
Notes	

October achievements

Be proud of yourself and all that you have achieved this month. Write down your wins, big and small. If you have not achieved everything that you set out to do, that's okay! We learn and grow through our mistakes and experiences. You can use this space to make notes about anything that you have learned.

November 2021

Notes	Monday	Tuesday	Wednesday
	1	2	3
	8	9	10
	15	16	17
	22	23	24
	29	30	1

Thursday	Friday	Saturday	Sunday
4 ●	5	6	7
11 ◗	12	13	14
18	19 ○	20	21
25	26	27 ◖	28
2	3	4	5

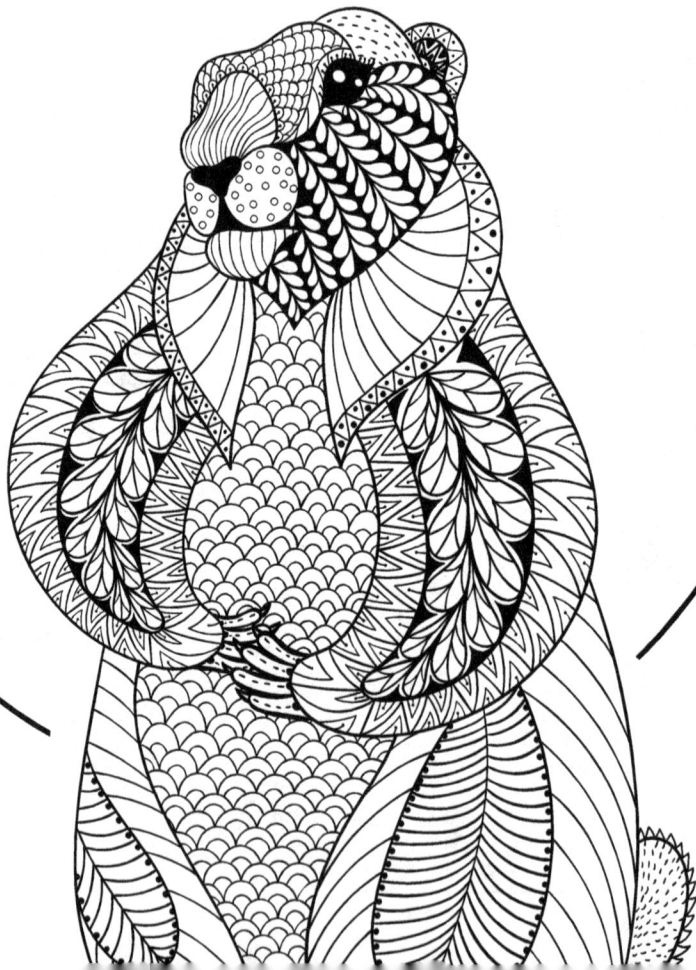

November

Beaver
moon

November goals

Use this space to write your goals for the month ahead, and any steps you can take that will get you to where you want to be.

'It does not matter how slowly you go, so long as you do not stop.'

— Confucius

Sometimes we get towards the end of the year and wonder how we got here. Time can seem to fly by so quickly. We may worry that we have not achieved everything we set out to do at the start of the year. Make a list of your main achievements in 2021. Whether growth has been fast or slow for you does not matter, you are heading in the right direction, and each step takes you closer to your destination.

Monday | 1 November 2021

6:00	**Today's quick wins**
7:00	
8:00	
9:00	
10:00	
11:00	**Health and nutrition**
12:00	
13:00	
14:00	**Today, I am grateful for...**
15:00	
16:00	
17:00	**Today's self care**
18:00	
19:00	
20:00	**Chart your cycle**
21:00	
22:00	
23:00	**Positive affirmation**
Notes	

Tuesday | 2 November 2021

6:00	**Today's quick wins**
7:00	
8:00	
9:00	
10:00	
11:00	**Health and nutrition**
12:00	
13:00	
14:00	**Today, I am grateful for...**
15:00	
16:00	
17:00	**Today's self care**
18:00	
19:00	
20:00	**Chart your cycle**
21:00	
22:00	
23:00	**Positive affirmation**
Notes	

Wednesday | 3 November 2021

6:00	
7:00	
8:00	
9:00	
10:00	
11:00	
12:00	
13:00	
14:00	
15:00	
16:00	
17:00	
18:00	
19:00	
20:00	
21:00	
22:00	
23:00	

Notes

Today's quick wins

Health and nutrition

Today, I am grateful for...

Today's self care

Chart your cycle

Positive affirmation

Thursday | 4 November 2021

6:00	**Today's quick wins**
7:00	
8:00	
9:00	
10:00	
11:00	**Health and nutrition**
12:00	
13:00	
14:00	**Today, I am grateful for...**
15:00	
16:00	
17:00	**Today's self care**
18:00	
19:00	
20:00	**Chart your cycle**
21:00	
22:00	
23:00	**Positive affirmation**
Notes	

Friday | 5 November 2021

6:00	**Today's quick wins**
7:00	
8:00	
9:00	
10:00	
11:00	**Health and nutrition**
12:00	
13:00	
14:00	**Today, I am grateful for...**
15:00	
16:00	
17:00	**Today's self care**
18:00	
19:00	
20:00	**Chart your cycle**
21:00	
22:00	
23:00	**Positive affirmation**
Notes	

Saturday | 6 November 2021

6:00	
7:00	
8:00	
9:00	
10:00	
11:00	
12:00	
13:00	
14:00	
15:00	
16:00	
17:00	
18:00	
19:00	
20:00	
21:00	
22:00	
23:00	

Today's quick wins

Health and nutrition

Today, I am grateful for...

Today's self care

Chart your cycle

Positive affirmation

Notes

Sunday | 7 November 2021

6:00	**Today's quick wins**
7:00	
8:00	
9:00	
10:00	
11:00	**Health and nutrition**
12:00	
13:00	
14:00	**Today, I am grateful for...**
15:00	
16:00	
17:00	**Today's self care**
18:00	
19:00	
20:00	**Chart your cycle**
21:00	
22:00	
23:00	**Positive affirmation**
Notes	

Monday | 8 November 2021

6:00	**Today's quick wins**
7:00	
8:00	
9:00	
10:00	
11:00	**Health and nutrition**
12:00	
13:00	
14:00	**Today, I am grateful for...**
15:00	
16:00	
17:00	**Today's self care**
18:00	
19:00	
20:00	**Chart your cycle**
21:00	
22:00	
23:00	**Positive affirmation**
Notes	

Tuesday | 9 November 2021

6:00	**Today's quick wins**
7:00	
8:00	
9:00	
10:00	
11:00	**Health and nutrition**
12:00	
13:00	
14:00	**Today, I am grateful for...**
15:00	
16:00	
17:00	**Today's self care**
18:00	
19:00	
20:00	**Chart your cycle**
21:00	
22:00	
23:00	**Positive affirmation**
Notes	

Wednesday | 10 November 2021

6:00	**Today's quick wins**
7:00	
8:00	
9:00	
10:00	
11:00	**Health and nutrition**
12:00	
13:00	
14:00	**Today, I am grateful for...**
15:00	
16:00	
17:00	**Today's self care**
18:00	
19:00	
20:00	**Chart your cycle**
21:00	
22:00	
23:00	**Positive affirmation**
Notes	

Thursday | 11 November 2021

6:00	**Today's quick wins**
7:00	
8:00	
9:00	
10:00	
11:00	**Health and nutrition**
12:00	
13:00	
14:00	**Today, I am grateful for...**
15:00	
16:00	
17:00	**Today's self care**
18:00	
19:00	
20:00	**Chart your cycle**
21:00	
22:00	
23:00	**Positive affirmation**
Notes	

Friday | 12 November 2021

6:00	
7:00	
8:00	
9:00	
10:00	
11:00	
12:00	
13:00	
14:00	
15:00	
16:00	
17:00	
18:00	
19:00	
20:00	
21:00	
22:00	
23:00	

Notes

Today's quick wins

Health and nutrition

Today, I am grateful for...

Today's self care

Chart your cycle

Positive affirmation

Saturday | 13 November 2021

6:00	**Today's quick wins**
7:00	
8:00	
9:00	
10:00	
11:00	**Health and nutrition**
12:00	
13:00	
14:00	**Today, I am grateful for...**
15:00	
16:00	
17:00	**Today's self care**
18:00	
19:00	
20:00	**Chart your cycle**
21:00	
22:00	
23:00	**Positive affirmation**

Notes

Sunday | 14 November 2021

6:00	**Today's quick wins**
7:00	
8:00	
9:00	
10:00	
11:00	**Health and nutrition**
12:00	
13:00	
14:00	**Today, I am grateful for...**
15:00	
16:00	
17:00	**Today's self care**
18:00	
19:00	
20:00	**Chart your cycle**
21:00	
22:00	
23:00	**Positive affirmation**
Notes	

Monday | 15 November 2021

6:00	**Today's quick wins**
7:00	
8:00	
9:00	
10:00	
11:00	**Health and nutrition**
12:00	
13:00	
14:00	**Today, I am grateful for...**
15:00	
16:00	
17:00	**Today's self care**
18:00	
19:00	
20:00	**Chart your cycle**
21:00	
22:00	
23:00	**Positive affirmation**
Notes	

Tuesday | 16 November 2021

6:00	**Today's quick wins**
7:00	
8:00	
9:00	
10:00	
11:00	**Health and nutrition**
12:00	
13:00	
14:00	**Today, I am grateful for...**
15:00	
16:00	
17:00	**Today's self care**
18:00	
19:00	
20:00	**Chart your cycle**
21:00	
22:00	
23:00	**Positive affirmation**
Notes	

Wednesday | 17 November 2021

6:00	**Today's quick wins**
7:00	
8:00	
9:00	
10:00	
11:00	**Health and nutrition**
12:00	
13:00	
14:00	**Today, I am grateful for...**
15:00	
16:00	
17:00	**Today's self care**
18:00	
19:00	
20:00	**Chart your cycle**
21:00	
22:00	
23:00	**Positive affirmation**
Notes	

Thursday | 18 November 2021

6:00	**Today's quick wins**
7:00	
8:00	
9:00	
10:00	
11:00	**Health and nutrition**
12:00	
13:00	
14:00	**Today, I am grateful for...**
15:00	
16:00	
17:00	**Today's self care**
18:00	
19:00	
20:00	**Chart your cycle**
21:00	
22:00	
23:00	**Positive affirmation**
Notes	

Friday | 19 November 2021

6:00	**Today's quick wins**
7:00	
8:00	
9:00	
10:00	
11:00	**Health and nutrition**
12:00	
13:00	
14:00	**Today, I am grateful for...**
15:00	
16:00	
17:00	**Today's self care**
18:00	
19:00	
20:00	**Chart your cycle**
21:00	
22:00	
23:00	**Positive affirmation**
Notes	

Saturday | 20 November 2021

6:00	**Today's quick wins**
7:00	
8:00	
9:00	
10:00	
11:00	**Health and nutrition**
12:00	
13:00	
14:00	**Today, I am grateful for...**
15:00	
16:00	
17:00	**Today's self care**
18:00	
19:00	
20:00	**Chart your cycle**
21:00	
22:00	
23:00	**Positive affirmation**
Notes	

Sunday | 21 November 2021

6:00	**Today's quick wins**
7:00	
8:00	
9:00	
10:00	
11:00	**Health and nutrition**
12:00	
13:00	
14:00	**Today, I am grateful for...**
15:00	
16:00	
17:00	**Today's self care**
18:00	
19:00	
20:00	**Chart your cycle**
21:00	
22:00	
23:00	**Positive affirmation**
Notes	

Monday | 22 November 2021

6:00	**Today's quick wins**
7:00	
8:00	
9:00	
10:00	
11:00	**Health and nutrition**
12:00	
13:00	
14:00	**Today, I am grateful for...**
15:00	
16:00	
17:00	**Today's self care**
18:00	
19:00	
20:00	**Chart your cycle**
21:00	
22:00	
23:00	**Positive affirmation**
Notes	

Tuesday | 23 November 2021

6:00	**Today's quick wins**
7:00	
8:00	
9:00	
10:00	
11:00	**Health and nutrition**
12:00	
13:00	
14:00	**Today, I am grateful for...**
15:00	
16:00	
17:00	**Today's self care**
18:00	
19:00	
20:00	**Chart your cycle**
21:00	
22:00	
23:00	**Positive affirmation**
Notes	

Wednesday | 24 November 2021

6:00	**Today's quick wins**
7:00	
8:00	
9:00	
10:00	
11:00	**Health and nutrition**
12:00	
13:00	
14:00	**Today, I am grateful for...**
15:00	
16:00	
17:00	**Today's self care**
18:00	
19:00	
20:00	**Chart your cycle**
21:00	
22:00	
23:00	**Positive affirmation**
Notes	

Thursday | 25 November 2021

6:00	**Today's quick wins**
7:00	
8:00	
9:00	
10:00	
11:00	**Health and nutrition**
12:00	
13:00	
14:00	**Today, I am grateful for...**
15:00	
16:00	
17:00	**Today's self care**
18:00	
19:00	
20:00	**Chart your cycle**
21:00	
22:00	
23:00	**Positive affirmation**
Notes	

Friday | 26 November 2021

6:00	
7:00	
8:00	
9:00	
10:00	
11:00	
12:00	
13:00	
14:00	
15:00	
16:00	
17:00	
18:00	
19:00	
20:00	
21:00	
22:00	
23:00	

Notes

Today's quick wins

Health and nutrition

Today, I am grateful for...

Today's self care

Chart your cycle

Positive affirmation

Saturday | 27 November 2021

6:00	**Today's quick wins**
7:00	
8:00	
9:00	
10:00	
11:00	**Health and nutrition**
12:00	
13:00	
14:00	**Today, I am grateful for...**
15:00	
16:00	
17:00	**Today's self care**
18:00	
19:00	
20:00	**Chart your cycle**
21:00	
22:00	
23:00	**Positive affirmation**
Notes	

Sunday | 28 November 2021

6:00	**Today's quick wins**
7:00	
8:00	
9:00	
10:00	
11:00	**Health and nutrition**
12:00	
13:00	
14:00	**Today, I am grateful for...**
15:00	
16:00	
17:00	**Today's self care**
18:00	
19:00	
20:00	**Chart your cycle**
21:00	
22:00	
23:00	**Positive affirmation**

Notes

Monday | 29 November 2021

6:00	
7:00	
8:00	
9:00	
10:00	
11:00	
12:00	
13:00	
14:00	
15:00	
16:00	
17:00	
18:00	
19:00	
20:00	
21:00	
22:00	
23:00	

Notes

Today's quick wins

Health and nutrition

Today, I am grateful for...

Today's self care

Chart your cycle

Positive affirmation

Tuesday | 30 November 2021

6:00	**Today's quick wins**
7:00	
8:00	
9:00	
10:00	
11:00	**Health and nutrition**
12:00	
13:00	
14:00	**Today, I am grateful for...**
15:00	
16:00	
17:00	**Today's self care**
18:00	
19:00	
20:00	**Chart your cycle**
21:00	
22:00	
23:00	**Positive affirmation**
Notes	

November achievements

Be proud of yourself and all that you have achieved this month. Write down your wins, big and small. If you have not achieved everything that you set out to do, that's okay! We learn and grow through our mistakes and experiences. You can use this space to make notes about anything that you have learned.

December 2021

Notes	Monday	Tuesday	Wednesday
	29	30	1
	6	7	8
	13	14	15
	20	21 *Winter solstice*	22
	27 ☽	28	29

Thursday	Friday	Saturday	Sunday
2	3	4 ●	5
9	10	11 ◐	12
16	17	18	19 ○
23	24	25	26
30	31	1	2

December

Cold moon

December goals

Use this space to write your goals for the month ahead, and any steps you can take that will get you to where you want to be.

Wednesday | 1 December 2021

6:00	**Today's quick wins**
7:00	
8:00	
9:00	
10:00	
11:00	**Health and nutrition**
12:00	
13:00	
14:00	**Today, I am grateful for...**
15:00	
16:00	
17:00	**Today's self care**
18:00	
19:00	
20:00	**Chart your cycle**
21:00	
22:00	
23:00	**Positive affirmation**
Notes	

Thursday | 2 December 2021

6:00	**Today's quick wins**
7:00	
8:00	
9:00	
10:00	
11:00	**Health and nutrition**
12:00	
13:00	
14:00	**Today, I am grateful for...**
15:00	
16:00	
17:00	**Today's self care**
18:00	
19:00	
20:00	**Chart your cycle**
21:00	
22:00	
23:00	**Positive affirmation**
Notes	

Friday | 3 December 2021

6:00	**Today's quick wins**
7:00	
8:00	
9:00	
10:00	
11:00	**Health and nutrition**
12:00	
13:00	
14:00	**Today, I am grateful for...**
15:00	
16:00	
17:00	**Today's self care**
18:00	
19:00	
20:00	**Chart your cycle**
21:00	
22:00	
23:00	**Positive affirmation**
Notes	

Saturday | 4 December 2021

6:00	**Today's quick wins**
7:00	
8:00	
9:00	
10:00	
11:00	**Health and nutrition**
12:00	
13:00	
14:00	**Today, I am grateful for...**
15:00	
16:00	
17:00	**Today's self care**
18:00	
19:00	
20:00	**Chart your cycle**
21:00	
22:00	
23:00	**Positive affirmation**
Notes	

Sunday | 5 December 2021

6:00	**Today's quick wins**
7:00	
8:00	
9:00	
10:00	
11:00	**Health and nutrition**
12:00	
13:00	
14:00	**Today, I am grateful for...**
15:00	
16:00	
17:00	**Today's self care**
18:00	
19:00	
20:00	**Chart your cycle**
21:00	
22:00	
23:00	**Positive affirmation**
Notes	

Monday | 6 December 2021

6:00	**Today's quick wins**
7:00	
8:00	
9:00	
10:00	
11:00	**Health and nutrition**
12:00	
13:00	
14:00	**Today, I am grateful for...**
15:00	
16:00	
17:00	**Today's self care**
18:00	
19:00	
20:00	**Chart your cycle**
21:00	
22:00	
23:00	**Positive affirmation**
Notes	

Tuesday | 7 December 2021

6:00	
7:00	
8:00	
9:00	
10:00	
11:00	
12:00	
13:00	
14:00	
15:00	
16:00	
17:00	
18:00	
19:00	
20:00	
21:00	
22:00	
23:00	

Notes

Today's quick wins

Health and nutrition

Today, I am grateful for...

Today's self care

Chart your cycle

Positive affirmation

Wednesday | 8 December 2021

6:00	**Today's quick wins**
7:00	
8:00	
9:00	
10:00	
11:00	**Health and nutrition**
12:00	
13:00	
14:00	**Today, I am grateful for...**
15:00	
16:00	
17:00	**Today's self care**
18:00	
19:00	
20:00	**Chart your cycle**
21:00	
22:00	
23:00	**Positive affirmation**
Notes	

Thursday | 9 December 2021

6:00	**Today's quick wins**
7:00	
8:00	
9:00	
10:00	
11:00	**Health and nutrition**
12:00	
13:00	
14:00	**Today, I am grateful for...**
15:00	
16:00	
17:00	**Today's self care**
18:00	
19:00	
20:00	**Chart your cycle**
21:00	
22:00	
23:00	**Positive affirmation**
Notes	

Friday | 10 December 2021

6:00	**Today's quick wins**
7:00	
8:00	
9:00	
10:00	
11:00	**Health and nutrition**
12:00	
13:00	
14:00	**Today, I am grateful for...**
15:00	
16:00	
17:00	**Today's self care**
18:00	
19:00	
20:00	**Chart your cycle**
21:00	
22:00	
23:00	**Positive affirmation**

Notes

Saturday | 11 December 2021

6:00	**Today's quick wins**
7:00	
8:00	
9:00	
10:00	
11:00	**Health and nutrition**
12:00	
13:00	
14:00	**Today, I am grateful for...**
15:00	
16:00	
17:00	**Today's self care**
18:00	
19:00	
20:00	**Chart your cycle**
21:00	
22:00	
23:00	**Positive affirmation**
Notes	

Sunday | 12 December 2021

6:00	**Today's quick wins**
7:00	
8:00	
9:00	
10:00	
11:00	**Health and nutrition**
12:00	
13:00	
14:00	**Today, I am grateful for...**
15:00	
16:00	
17:00	**Today's self care**
18:00	
19:00	
20:00	**Chart your cycle**
21:00	
22:00	
23:00	**Positive affirmation**
Notes	

Monday | 13 December 2021

6:00	**Today's quick wins**
7:00	
8:00	
9:00	
10:00	
11:00	**Health and nutrition**
12:00	
13:00	
14:00	**Today, I am grateful for...**
15:00	
16:00	
17:00	**Today's self care**
18:00	
19:00	
20:00	**Chart your cycle**
21:00	
22:00	
23:00	**Positive affirmation**
Notes	

Tuesday | 14 December 2021

6:00	**Today's quick wins**
7:00	
8:00	
9:00	
10:00	
11:00	**Health and nutrition**
12:00	
13:00	
14:00	**Today, I am grateful for...**
15:00	
16:00	
17:00	**Today's self care**
18:00	
19:00	
20:00	**Chart your cycle**
21:00	
22:00	
23:00	**Positive affirmation**

Notes

Wednesday | 15 December 2021

6:00	
7:00	
8:00	
9:00	
10:00	
11:00	
12:00	
13:00	
14:00	
15:00	
16:00	
17:00	
18:00	
19:00	
20:00	
21:00	
22:00	
23:00	

Today's quick wins

Health and nutrition

Today, I am grateful for...

Today's self care

Chart your cycle

Positive affirmation

Notes

Thursday | 16 December 2021

6:00	
7:00	
8:00	
9:00	
10:00	
11:00	
12:00	
13:00	
14:00	
15:00	
16:00	
17:00	
18:00	
19:00	
20:00	
21:00	
22:00	
23:00	

Today's quick wins

Health and nutrition

Today, I am grateful for...

Today's self care

Chart your cycle

Positive affirmation

Notes

Friday | 17 December 2021

6:00	**Today's quick wins**
7:00	
8:00	
9:00	
10:00	
11:00	**Health and nutrition**
12:00	
13:00	
14:00	**Today, I am grateful for...**
15:00	
16:00	
17:00	**Today's self care**
18:00	
19:00	
20:00	**Chart your cycle**
21:00	
22:00	
23:00	**Positive affirmation**
Notes	

Saturday | 18 December 2021

6:00	**Today's quick wins**
7:00	
8:00	
9:00	
10:00	
11:00	**Health and nutrition**
12:00	
13:00	
14:00	**Today, I am grateful for...**
15:00	
16:00	
17:00	**Today's self care**
18:00	
19:00	
20:00	**Chart your cycle**
21:00	
22:00	
23:00	**Positive affirmation**
Notes	

Sunday | 19 December 2021

6:00	**Today's quick wins**
7:00	
8:00	
9:00	
10:00	
11:00	**Health and nutrition**
12:00	
13:00	
14:00	**Today, I am grateful for...**
15:00	
16:00	
17:00	**Today's self care**
18:00	
19:00	
20:00	**Chart your cycle**
21:00	
22:00	
23:00	**Positive affirmation**

Notes

Monday | 20 December 2021

6:00	**Today's quick wins**
7:00	
8:00	
9:00	
10:00	
11:00	**Health and nutrition**
12:00	
13:00	
14:00	**Today, I am grateful for...**
15:00	
16:00	
17:00	**Today's self care**
18:00	
19:00	
20:00	**Chart your cycle**
21:00	
22:00	
23:00	**Positive affirmation**
Notes	

Tuesday | 21 December 2021 - *Winter solstice*

6:00	**Today's quick wins**
7:00	
8:00	
9:00	
10:00	
11:00	**Health and nutrition**
12:00	
13:00	
14:00	**Today, I am grateful for...**
15:00	
16:00	
17:00	**Today's self care**
18:00	
19:00	
20:00	**Chart your cycle**
21:00	
22:00	
23:00	**Positive affirmation**
Notes	

Wednesday | 22 December 2021

6:00	**Today's quick wins**
7:00	
8:00	
9:00	
10:00	
11:00	**Health and nutrition**
12:00	
13:00	
14:00	**Today, I am grateful for...**
15:00	
16:00	
17:00	**Today's self care**
18:00	
19:00	
20:00	**Chart your cycle**
21:00	
22:00	
23:00	**Positive affirmation**
Notes	

Thursday | 23 December 2021

6:00	**Today's quick wins**
7:00	
8:00	
9:00	
10:00	
11:00	**Health and nutrition**
12:00	
13:00	
14:00	**Today, I am grateful for...**
15:00	
16:00	
17:00	**Today's self care**
18:00	
19:00	
20:00	**Chart your cycle**
21:00	
22:00	
23:00	**Positive affirmation**
Notes	

Friday | 24 December 2021

6:00	**Today's quick wins**
7:00	
8:00	
9:00	
10:00	
11:00	**Health and nutrition**
12:00	
13:00	
14:00	**Today, I am grateful for...**
15:00	
16:00	
17:00	**Today's self care**
18:00	
19:00	
20:00	**Chart your cycle**
21:00	
22:00	
23:00	**Positive affirmation**
Notes	

Saturday | 25 December 2021

6:00	
7:00	
8:00	
9:00	
10:00	
11:00	
12:00	
13:00	
14:00	
15:00	
16:00	
17:00	
18:00	
19:00	
20:00	
21:00	
22:00	
23:00	

Notes

Today's quick wins

Health and nutrition

Today, I am grateful for...

Today's self care

Chart your cycle

Positive affirmation

Sunday | 26 December 2021

6:00	**Today's quick wins**
7:00	
8:00	
9:00	
10:00	
11:00	**Health and nutrition**
12:00	
13:00	
14:00	**Today, I am grateful for...**
15:00	
16:00	
17:00	**Today's self care**
18:00	
19:00	
20:00	**Chart your cycle**
21:00	
22:00	
23:00	**Positive affirmation**

Notes

Monday | 27 December 2021

6:00	**Today's quick wins**
7:00	
8:00	
9:00	
10:00	
11:00	**Health and nutrition**
12:00	
13:00	
14:00	**Today, I am grateful for...**
15:00	
16:00	
17:00	**Today's self care**
18:00	
19:00	
20:00	**Chart your cycle**
21:00	
22:00	
23:00	**Positive affirmation**
Notes	

Tuesday | 28 December 2021

6:00	**Today's quick wins**
7:00	
8:00	
9:00	
10:00	
11:00	**Health and nutrition**
12:00	
13:00	
14:00	**Today, I am grateful for...**
15:00	
16:00	
17:00	**Today's self care**
18:00	
19:00	
20:00	**Chart your cycle**
21:00	
22:00	
23:00	**Positive affirmation**
Notes	

Wednesday | 29 December 2021

6:00	**Today's quick wins**
7:00	
8:00	
9:00	
10:00	
11:00	**Health and nutrition**
12:00	
13:00	
14:00	**Today, I am grateful for...**
15:00	
16:00	
17:00	**Today's self care**
18:00	
19:00	
20:00	**Chart your cycle**
21:00	
22:00	
23:00	**Positive affirmation**
Notes	

Thursday | 30 December 2021

6:00	**Today's quick wins**
7:00	
8:00	
9:00	
10:00	
11:00	**Health and nutrition**
12:00	
13:00	
14:00	**Today, I am grateful for...**
15:00	
16:00	
17:00	**Today's self care**
18:00	
19:00	
20:00	**Chart your cycle**
21:00	
22:00	
23:00	**Positive affirmation**
Notes	

Friday | 31 December 2021

6:00	**Today's quick wins**
7:00	
8:00	
9:00	
10:00	
11:00	**Health and nutrition**
12:00	
13:00	
14:00	**Today, I am grateful for...**
15:00	
16:00	
17:00	**Today's self care**
18:00	
19:00	
20:00	**Chart your cycle**
21:00	
22:00	
23:00	**Positive affirmation**
Notes	

December achievements

Be proud of yourself and all that you have achieved this month. Write down your wins, big and small. If you have not achieved everything that you set out to do, that's okay! We learn and grow through our mistakes and experiences. You can use this space to make notes about anything that you have learned.

What have I achieved and how
have I grown in 2021...

Books, films and quotes
to remember...

Notes

Notes

Notes

Further reading

To learn more about working with the cycles of the moon
- Lunar Living by Kirsty Gallagher

To learn about charting and working in harmony with your cycle
- Code Red by Lisa Lister and In Flo by Alisa Vitti

To learn about manifesting
- Creative Visualization by Shakti Gawain
- The Power of Intention by Dr Wayne Dyer
- Ask and it is Given by Jerry and Esther Hicks
- Becoming Supernatural by Dr Joe Dispenza

To learn about Spiritual Inspiration
- The Seven Spiritual Laws of Success by Deepak Chopra
- The Power of Now by Eckhart Tolle
- The Four Agreements by Miguel Ruiz
- Be here Now by Ram Das
- Tao Te Ching by Lao Tzu

To learn about Healthy living
- You Can Heal Your Life by Louise Hay
- And Breathe by Rebecca Dennis
- Eat Feel Fresh by Sahara Rose Kitabi

To learn about Healing Creative Blocks
- The Artists Way by Julia Cameron

www.ingramcontent.com/pod-product-compliance
Lightning Source LLC
Chambersburg PA
CBHW071939260326

41914CB00004B/677

9 781527 277717